Taylor,

I really appreciate you
+ love you BIG!

♡
Kristy

This journal belongs to

....

ISBN 978-1-64352-899-1

Published by Barbour Publishing, Inc., 1810 Barbour Drive, Uhrichsville, Ohio 44683, www.barbourbooks.com

Our mission is to inspire the world with the life-changing message of the Bible.

Member of the
Evangelical Christian
Publishers Association

Printed in China.

Donna K.
Maltese

More
Jesus

A Devotional Journal

What Your Heart Needs
for the Hard Days

BARBOUR
PUBLISHING

Just What Your Heart Needs. . .
More Jesus

*W*ithin the following pages, you'll find more than one hundred readings to help grow your faith, hope, and trust in God. Written specifically for those times when your inner woman cries out for more wisdom, more energy, more guidance—more *everything*—More Jesus will fill your heart with all the strength you need to face those not-so-easy days.

Jesus' mother, Mary, took good care of her own heart—the center of her physical and spiritual life. She paid attention to the things said about her Son, the words He spoke, and the events that shaped their lives. She pondered, meditated on, and treasured them—*in her heart* (Luke 2:19, 51). Believing women would be wise to follow her lead: to read God's Word, listen to Jesus, and allow the Spirit to guide their inner selves into truth.

To that end, each devotional reading includes a Bible verse and a prayer. Then, to help you store up God's riches deep within your inner self, a "Heart Treasure" provides a takeaway spiritual truth to ponder throughout your day, to feed and guard your heart. Nurturing your heart in this way will lead you closer to God, bring you more in tune with the Spirit, and enable you to find more Jesus.

My child, pay attention to what I say. Listen carefully to my words. Don't lose sight of them. Let them penetrate deep into your heart, for they bring life to those who find them, and healing to their whole body. Guard your heart above all else, for it determines the course of your life.
Proverbs 4:20–23 nlt

5

Finding Soul Rest

*Take My yoke upon you and learn of Me, for I am gentle (meek)
and humble (lowly) in heart, and you will find rest (relief and ease
and refreshment and recreation and blessed quiet) for your souls.*
MATTHEW 11:29 AMPC

$\mathcal{S}$ome mornings we wake up feeling weighed down with a burden. Perhaps we're carrying something over from the day before. Or our thoughts are careening around as we consider all the tasks that lie before us. Maybe a nameless foreboding sneaks up on us, leading us into worry.

Or instead of coming upon us at daybreak, perhaps the burden invades our being at midday or even at night, sinking us even deeper into our pillows yet keeping us from the sleep we need.

Whatever our burden (known or nameless) and whenever it comes (morning, noon, or night), we need not despair but merely reach out to the great burden bearer, Jesus. He invites us to go outside ourselves and into Him, saying, "Come to me. Get away with me and you'll recover your life. I'll show you how to take a real rest" (Matthew 11:28 MSG). And He doesn't stop there. He says, "Walk with me and work with me—watch how I do it. Learn the unforced rhythms of grace" (verse 29 MSG).

What a concept! What a break! All we need to do is go to Jesus. Lay down our burdens—our wills, ideas, worries, fears, nameless forebodings, or whatever weights are bowing us down—at His feet. And then take Him up on His further invitation: "Keep company with me and you'll learn to live freely and lightly" (verse 30 MSG). What a prescription for relief!

So now that we know our malady (a burden) and the remedy (going to Jesus and resting in Him), how do we get there from here? We stop in our tracks—no matter when, no matter where. We get out of our own heads. We replace the thoughts careening around in our minds with the words of Jesus. We ask Him to take upon Himself our load of care—whether or not we can name it. And we ask Him to replace it with exactly what we need: more of Him—His light, His presence, His peace. In so doing, we find true rest for our souls.

Lord, I'm feeling so burdened today. So I'm taking these moments to stop and come to You. To get away with You. Help me recover the life You want me to live. Replace my anxieties with the rest and peace only You can provide for me. Take me out of myself and lift me into You. In Your name I pray, amen.

Heart Treasure: In Jesus, I find rest for my soul.

....

....

....

....

....

....

....

....

....

....

....

....

....

....

Finding Inspiration and Bounty

Simon Peter said, "I'm going fishing." "We'll come, too," they all said.
So they went out in the boat, but they caught nothing all night.
JOHN 21:3 NLT

You have a job—whether it's inside the house or outside. Something you put your hand to. Perhaps you're a stay-at-home mom, or a freelancer with a home office, or you go out to your job every day, only to return home to more duties. Regardless of what you do, you are about the business of doing. And for some reason, as you go about your tasks, nothing is working out. You feel as if you are reaping nothing from all your hard work. You keep coming up empty, which brings about disappointment.

And then you hear a voice. Jesus' voice, although you may not yet recognize it as His. It may come as an idea, a thought. But it's there. And you obey. You follow the directive.

Suddenly you have success where there was none before! You draw up your net and find it overflowing with fish! Gradually you realize that the thought or idea you had wasn't yours at all. It was Christ's! You see Him standing on the shore of your mind, smiling. You see Him waving you in to the beach where He already has a fire started, looking forward to you joining Him and sharing in the bounty.

So glad are you to see Him, so overjoyed are you at obeying Him and reaping the amazing benefits, you rush to meet Him, to celebrate with Him, to commune with Him.

Know that Jesus is always nearer than you think. He's continually watching out from the shore, wanting to give you direction if only you'd listen when He yells out. If only you'd recognize that all your success comes from His hand, the hand of your Master Provider.

Rather than succumbing to a sense of loss or disappointment, open your mind to the voice of the One who has your best interests at heart. The One who wants to see that you are making your way, providing for yourself and others in your life. Obey the voice that calls out from the shore, giving you direction—in all areas of life. And then recognize that what you gain—in fact, all that you have—is from the hand of God, the One who knows everything, even where all the fish are.

Jesus, I am opening my mind and heart to You today in all the tasks that lie before me. As I go about my daily duties, may I hear—and obey—all the advice You have to give. May I realize that all the ideas I have, all the inspiration I receive, come from You. And may I join with You as we celebrate the bounty Your words have provided! Amen.

Heart Treasure: In Jesus, I find inspiration and bounty.

Finding All You Need

You can be sure that God will take care of everything you need,
his generosity exceeding even yours in the glory that pours from Jesus.
PHILIPPIANS 4:19 MSG

What are you looking for? Perhaps it's a job. Maybe a husband. Or it could be a house. It may seem like you've been looking forever, wondering when your need or want will be fulfilled. And the questions are racing around in your head. Regarding a job, you ask yourself, *How far am I willing to commute for a new position? Do I want to relocate? Should I relocate?* Regarding a potential spouse, you may ask, *How do I go about this? Should I go online? What exactly do I want in a husband? What should he look like? How old should he be?* If a house is what you're looking for, your questions might sound like, *How far am I willing to move away from my church or family? How big a house do I want? Is it time to downsize?* And in the midst of all the uncertainty, you ask God, *When? When will this happen? When will my search be over? How long do I look before I just give up? What do You think, Lord?*

Now is the time you may want to consider that you already have everything you really need. His name is Jesus. He wants to be your occupation, to "occupy" your time. He wants to love and adore you as your Husband. And He wants to be your home.

Granted, all the questions you've been asking yourself are valid. They are all things that should be considered. The problem arises when you begin feeling overwhelmed, so preoccupied with finding the answers to your questions, with finding the perfect job, man, or home, that you miss out on what Jesus is so ready to give you: peace, contentment, grounding.

The apostle Paul had it right when he said that God will provide more than what you need through His Son, Jesus.

Now that you have been reminded of that fact, that truth, how do you realize it in your life? Simple. When the overwhelming uncertainties start overtaking you, take a deep breath. Then fill in the blank: "Jesus, You alone are my _____." And believe what you say. As you do so, Jesus' all-surpassing peace will settle upon you. You will find your focus shift from what and who you *don't* have to what and who you *do* have with Jesus in your life.

> *Lord, I have so many questions. I want to know today what will be provided tomorrow. I don't like this feeling of uncertainty. It's clouding my thinking and keeping me from seeing what I do have in You. So I'm coming to You in this moment for peace, contentment, and grounding. For You alone are my _____.*

Heart Treasure: In Jesus, I find all I need.

Finding Forgiveness

"In prayer there is a connection between what God does and what you do. You can't get forgiveness from God, for instance, without also forgiving others. If you refuse to do your part, you cut yourself off from God's part."
MATTHEW 6:14–15 MSG

he words people speak have a tremendous amount of power over us. When those words are loving or uplifting, we feel their warmth, their inspiration. But when those words are cruel, we feel as if we've been struck, slapped on the face, punched in the stomach, the wind knocked out of us.

Yet it's not just words that hold sway over us. The actions of others impact us as well. Some sorts of physical contact or even just certain looks we get from others can leave us reeling, wondering what we did to deserve them.

When we've been injured by either the words or the actions of others, a feeling of bitterness can take root if we don't forgive the perpetrators. And, as we know, bitterness has a tendency to grow into resentment. But that's not the only problem that may arise. Jesus says that when we don't forgive those who have wronged us—no matter the weight of that wrong—God will not forgive us. So begins a disconnect between us and our Creator when we go to Him in prayer.

The remedy to this problem is, of course, to forgive—no matter how grievous the wrong. And not just a surface "Okay, I forgive that person." It must go much deeper. Jesus says you must "freely forgive your brother from your heart his offenses" (Matthew 18:35 AMPC). God is concerned about your heart. That's where He has His eyes.

Thus, you are to forgive as you hope to be forgiven. Moreover, you are to hold no malice toward your offenders, just as God holds no malice toward you but rather wants the best for you.

Now that you know what to do, how can you do it? Try this.

The next time you find it hard to forgive someone, think back to a time when you did something that offended another person, whether by word or deed. Hopefully, it was something you took to God, left at His feet, and asked Him to forgive. Remember how grateful you were when God extended His mercy to you. Then go and do the same, saving both yourself *and* your offender.

Lord Jesus, search me. Reveal to me the areas in my life where I am holding grudges. Help me to go deep, all the way to my heart, and forgive any who have harmed me in some way. Build up in me a willingness, a desire, to reach out to them. And to do so in Your loving name. Amen.

Heart Treasure: In Jesus, I forgive and am forgiven.

....

....

....

....

....

....

....

....

....

....

....

....

....

Finding Your Vision

So Jesus laid hands on his eyes again. The man looked hard and realized that he had recovered perfect sight, saw everything in bright, twenty-twenty focus.
MARK 8:25 MSG

*Y*ou had a path, a vision of where you thought the Lord wanted you to go. But now you're not so sure. Perhaps you're so caught up in the daily doings of life that your vision has faded. Or maybe circumstances have led you away from your initial path, and now you feel directionless. In fact, you feel confused. Not only that, but you've neglected to consult Jesus, to ask Him to help you get refocused. After you talk to others about your quandary, they lead you to Him. "That's where you should be looking for help," they say.

Unfocused, uncertain, directionless, you are like the sightless man at Bethsaida (Mark 8:22–26). His friends brought him to Jesus and asked Him to restore the blind man's sight.

What is the first thing Jesus does? He leads the man away from others. Out of the village. Away to a solitary place. It's just Jesus and the sightless one. Then Jesus applies an extremely personal touch. "He put spit in the man's eyes, laid hands on him, and asked, 'Do you see anything?' " (Mark 8:23 MSG).

The man looks up and answers that, yes, he sees something. He sees men. But they look like trees walking. The blind man's dormant faith has been aroused by the miracle of partial sight. Enough so that Jesus bolsters his burgeoning belief by laying His hands on the man's eyes again. It's at that point, with full-fledged faith in the Miracle Worker standing before him, that the man suddenly realizes he now has perfect vision. And Jesus sends him the way He wants him to go.

It's okay if you've temporarily lost your way. Now you know what to do. Go to a solitary place. A place where you can be alone with Jesus. Once there, ask Him to restore your vision. To open your eyes to what He would have you see and do. As you do so, the more He will make things clear to you and the more your faith will grow. And as it grows, you'll know just where He wants you to go and be, to see and do, each step of the way.

Lord, I feel as if I've lost my direction. I'm not sure which way to go. So I'm coming to You, Jesus. It's just You and me alone, in this solitary place. Put Your hands upon my eyes. Restore the vision You have for my life. And if things aren't clear at first, continue to grow my faith as You touch my life. Help me to see what You're doing and to go the way You'd have me go. Amen.

Heart Treasure: In Jesus, I find my vision.

Finding the Words You Need

*But Jesus told him, "No! The Scriptures say, 'People do not live by bread
alone, but by every word that comes from the mouth of God.' "*
MATTHEW 4:4 NLT

*J*ust one more cookie. After all, what could it hurt?

Perhaps cookies aren't a temptation for you. Maybe your thoughts are
more like, *Just one more minute on Facebook. Then I'll get back to work.* Or
Why not have a cigarette? What could one hurt? Or *He's almost separated.
Why not go on a date with him?*

Yes, temptations are many and varied. And they often have dire
consequences—if not now, sometime later. So what's a woman to do?
Simple: follow Jesus' example.

In Matthew 4:4, we read the second sentence Jesus uttered in that
Gospel. It came out of His mouth after He'd spent forty days and forty
nights fasting in the wilderness. And He said it in response to Satan's
challenge, "If you're God's Son, turn these stones into loaves of bread"
(see Matthew 4:3).

Jesus came back quoting Deuteronomy 8:3, saying, "It's not bread
alone that people need for nourishment. They need the spiritual food that
comes from God's mouth."

Two more times, Satan tried to manipulate Jesus, to tempt Him into
doing something that would go against God's plan for saving the world
from sin. And both times Jesus countered with a word against temptation, a
quote from the Old Testament (the only Bible Jesus and His early followers
had), beginning each of His quotes with phrases like, "The Scriptures
say. . ." or "It is written. . ."—both of which are a reference to God's Word.
At the end of the story, "the devil went away, and angels came and took
care of Jesus" (Matthew 4:11 NLT).

This account is powerful. For it not only reveals that the Word equips believers with a weapon against evil forces (Ephesians 6:17), but shows Christ followers where they can go for spiritual nourishment, power, and strength whenever and wherever they need it.

Yet to be able to fight temptation, to use the Word as your weapon, to acquire the strength, power, and nourishment it affords, you need to dig into both the Old and New Testaments. And go deep. Allow it to seep into your system, to become part of who you are, so that when temptation does rear its head, you have a ready response to repel its effects. "For the word of God is alive and powerful" (Hebrews 4:12 NLT).

Jesus, I want to delve into God's Word. As I do so, reveal what You would have me know and memorize. Through Your Holy Spirit, give me the understanding I need so I can go deep and get the nourishment to better stand up against those things that come against me. I pray this in Your name, Jesus. Amen.

Heart Treasure: In Jesus, I find the words I need.

Finding God with You

An angel of the Lord appeared to him [Joseph] in a dream. . . .
"Do not be afraid to take Mary as your wife. For the child within
her was conceived by the Holy Spirit. And she will have a son, and you
are to name him Jesus, for he will save his people from their sins."
MATTHEW 1:20–21 NLT

*W*hat a great plan God had for us! God brought Jesus into this world so that He could show us who God is and how He wants us to live, and so that Jesus could become the go-between between us and Father God. Yet He also brought Jesus into our *lives* so He could *save* us. Yes, save us! From ourselves, our sins, and the wily schemes of others. Jesus came and died for us so that we could live—forever with Father God!

But that's not all! Jesus—the earthly representation of His Father—arrived so that *God* could be *with us*. That's one of the names Jesus was given, just as the prophets predicted: "Behold, the virgin shall become pregnant and give birth to a Son, and they shall call His name Emmanuel, which, when translated, means, God with us" (Matthew 1:23 AMPC).

Wow! What a blessing! This changes everything!

No matter what's going on in your life, you can know and remember that God is with you. But that's not enough, really. You must believe it. You must have *faith* that God is with you. That no matter where you are or where you go, He is not just by your side but within, above, below. He goes before you to pave the way ahead. He steps between you and things that could harm you. He lifts you up, moves you, takes you into Himself.

So don't be afraid. Know that you have a Savior, a rescuer, in your life. He's there to be with you through thick and thin. And that's *not* a dream—it's your reality. Your job is to live it.

Begin by taking a moment each day to breathe in the presence of God. To recognize that God is indeed with and within you. For as Jesus said, "I am in my Father, and you are in me, and I am in you" (John 14:20

NLT). No matter what comes against you, you're not alone. For the God within you is there for life—eternal life.

Emmanuel, God with me, You are a blessing in my life. Beyond what I ever could have hoped or imagined. And this is no dream. It's reality. Help me keep Your presence in my heart, mind, soul, and spirit as I go through my day. For when I know it as my truth, Your truth for me, I can face anything. Amen.

Heart Treasure: In Jesus, I find God with me.

....

....

....

....

....

....

....

....

....

....

....

....

....

....

Finding the True Kingdom

"You're blessed when you're at the end of your rope.
With less of you there is more of God and his rule."
MATTHEW 5:3 MSG

$\mathcal{M}$any of Jesus' teachings turn the world as we know it upside down. But at the same time, they turn us right-side up!

In Matthew 5, Jesus goes on top of a mountain to give the crowd a lesson on what God is looking for in His people. The first "be-attitude" that Jesus comes out with is "You're blessed when you're at the end of your rope. With less of you there is more of God and his rule."

What a concept! Jesus is saying that when you don't know where to turn, when you've lost more than you realized you ever had, you are blessed! How can that be?

When Paul was at a very low point in his life, he wrote, "I have learned the secret of living in every situation, whether it is with a full stomach or empty, with plenty or little. For I can do everything through Christ, who gives me strength" (Philippians 4:12–13 NLT). He knew that the weaker he became, the more the power of Christ moved in him (2 Corinthians 12:7–10).

While the world goes on hungering for more power, money, material things, status, and so on, we're to know we're blessed, prosperous daughters of the King because we have more of Christ in our lives! More of God's power within us.

The New Living Translation puts Matthew 5:3 this way: "God blesses those who are poor and realize their need for him, for the Kingdom of Heaven is theirs." What more riches do we need than to have Christ within us, leading us into the kingdom of heaven, and the Holy Spirit helping us to understand how to get there from here!

So, okay. You're at the end of your rope. You're thinking you've got nowhere else to turn. But Jesus is saying that you're exactly where you need to be. You're at the place where there's less of you and more of God. That means He is there to fill you up, to give you the joy you need to live the life He wants you to live. To be the woman He created you to be. In Jesus, you're no longer at the end of your rope—you're at the beginning of His.

Jesus, thanks for turning the world upside down and leaving me right-side up with Your words. In You, I know I have the strength I need and the joy I crave to live this life with You. Help me to keep this attitude of contentment—no matter what my circumstances—as I go through my day, knowing that regardless of how things may seem, I'm a daughter of the King. Amen.

Heart Treasure: In Jesus, I find the true kingdom.

....
....
....
....
....
....
....
....
....
....
....
....
....
....

Finding Peace

*Peace I leave with you; My [own] peace I now give and bequeath
to you. Not as the world gives do I give to you. Do not let your hearts
be troubled, neither let them be afraid. [Stop allowing yourselves
to be agitated and disturbed; and do not permit yourselves to
be fearful and intimidated and cowardly and unsettled.]*
JOHN 14:27 AMPC

Today more than ever we find ourselves upset, disturbed, out of sorts, in despair from the news we hear of wars, threats, terrorist attacks, shootings, hurricanes, cyclones, tornadoes, tsunamis, diseases, and more. We hear it. We see it. It comes into our in-boxes, blips on our phones, headlines our newspapers, gets delivered to us nonstop on a daily basis.

So how does a woman keep not only her peace but her sanity? How does she keep herself out of the world's darkness and in the light of Jesus? She goes to, holds on to, has faith in, and implements the sage advice the apostle Paul gives: "You'll do best by filling your minds and meditating on things true, noble, reputable, authentic, compelling, gracious—the best, not the worst; the beautiful, not the ugly; things to praise, not things to curse" (Philippians 4:8 MSG).

That may mean skipping the newspaper headlines and heading right to the comics. It may mean not watching the news. Perhaps it will mean getting off your Twitter account. Or taking more care in what you're watching on TV.

What it definitely means is spending more time reading, listening to, or watching things that inspire. Pick up and read your Bible more. Immerse yourself in the Psalms. Settle into the wisdom of Proverbs. And then meditate, thinking about all the good things in life. Take a walk outside and enjoy the nature God has provided.

No, you shouldn't ignore all that's happening in the world. It's good to be aware, to stay informed, to know where God may want you to step in, help out, play a part. But it's not good to allow all the bad things that are going on to depress you to the point where you can't even lift your head or you feel too unsettled to walk out the door.

Don't let the bad news consume you to the point where you miss out on what God wants you to do. Step out of the world and dip into God, His Good News, His peace, His Son.

Jesus, I so long for Your peace and light in this world. Help me to step away from the bad news that at times engulfs me. And help me to step into Your Word. To step out into nature. To absorb all the good that is God. In doing so, I know I'll gain the strength and power of Your presence and discover what You'd have me do to spread Your light and life.

Heart Treasure: In Jesus, I find my peace.

Finding God's Good Intent

"You intended to harm me, but God intended it all for good.
He brought me to this position so I could save the lives of many people."
GENESIS 50:20 NLT

*I*n the Old Testament are "types of Christ," people whose character or actions resemble those of Jesus in the New Testament. One such type is Joseph. And oh, the troubles he'd seen.

Things for Joseph started out well enough. He was his father's favorite. The downside was his older brothers knew it and hated him for it. So much so that they threw him into a pit and sold him to slave traders. Then they went back to their father, Jacob, with Joseph's tailor-made, now-shredded, bloodied coat of many colors in hand, reporting that wild animals had killed the boy.

Long story short, Joseph was bought as a slave in Egypt, accused of rape, and locked in a dungeon. Eventually he was called up from the depths to translate a dream for Pharaoh, who, because of Joseph's dream-interpretation abilities and general wisdom, made him overseer of the kingdom! When Joseph met up again with his brothers, he said something like this: "No need to fear. No worries. Although you did what you could with the intent of harming me, God worked it all out for good." And then he added: "Don't be afraid. I will continue to take care of you and your children" (Genesis 50:21 NLT).

What forgiveness! Just like that of Jesus! But how did Joseph get there?

No matter where Joseph was or what role he was playing, the Lord was with him. Even though he was separated from his family, friends, and dreams, the knowledge that he was not separated from God was a great comfort to Joseph. Even though Joseph was a slave, wrongly accused, and imprisoned, God was there, working things out for the good of him and many others, and even making him *prosper* (Genesis 39)!

Maybe your situation isn't as low as Joseph's or your dreams as high. But know this: no matter what you're going through, no matter how desperate the situation, no matter how many dreams seem scattered to the dust, God is with you. Take that knowledge to heart. Have faith that wherever and whoever you are, God can make you prosper. God intends—and is already orchestrating (although it may not seem like it on the surface)—all things to work out for your good.

*Lord Jesus, I'm not sure why certain things have happened,
but I know Father God intends everything to work for the good of
me and those around me. No matter where I am or the role I'm playing,
remind me that You're with me. And in the comfort of that knowledge,
remind me that You'll give me all the success I need. In Jesus' name I pray.*

Heart Treasure: In Jesus, I know God is with me,
intending all things for my good.

Finding Comfort and Regaining Hope

*"How happy are those who know what sorrow means
for they will be given courage and comfort!"*
MATTHEW 5:4 PHILLIPS

*A*t some point in our lives, we will suffer some sort of loss. It may be a close family member, a job, a house, an opportunity, or a dream. And we mourn such a loss. We cry over what could've been. We find ourselves shaken to our core, knowing our lives will never be the same. And if one more person says we'll adjust to a "new normal," we think we'll scream. Because as we're attempting to adjust, still reeling from our loss, we see all those around us going on with their lives as normal.

That's when Jesus steps in and says, "How happy are those who know what sorrow means for they will be given courage and comfort!" Or, as *The Message* puts it, "You're blessed when you feel you've lost what is most dear to you. Only then can you be embraced by the One most dear to you."

When you're in the midst of your grief, those words may not help. They may not even get through to you, so dark is the cloud in which you're engulfed. Yet eventually they'll find a way in and you'll realize their truth.

Remember Job? When he lost everything, he said, "GOD gives, GOD takes. God's name be ever blessed" (Job 1:21 MSG). That's a pretty good attitude after losing his home, animals, wealth, livelihood, and children. And on top of that, "not once did he blame God" (Job 1:22 MSG). Even when Job's health declined to the point where he was sitting in ashes, using shards from a broken pot to scrape the itching, oozing sores on his body, and his wife advised, "Curse God and be done with it!" (Job 2:9 MSG), Job remained firm in his faith, telling her, "We take the good days from God—why not also the bad days?" (Job 2:10 MSG).

That's to be our attitude when we encounter a loss. As Christians, we gain even more strength by remembering that if we have Jesus, we haven't really lost anything. In fact, we take heart, knowing that somehow God will make good come from all this (Romans 8:28).

Although you may not yet see what good God has in store for you, go to Him to get the comfort you need. And rely on your faith to carry you through.

Lord Jesus, pour out Your comfort, love, peace, and strength upon me. Hold me close in Your arms. Lift me up out of this darkness and into the warmth of Your light. As I commune with You, remind me that You'll make something good come out of my circumstances. Help me to hold on to that truth, that hope, as I once again find my footing in You.

Heart Treasure: In Jesus, I find comfort and regain hope.

Finding the Light

The waters compassed me about, even to [the extinction of] life;
the abyss surrounded me, the seaweed was wrapped about my head.
I went down to the bottoms and the very roots of the mountains;
the earth with its bars closed behind me forever.
JONAH 2:5–6 AMPC

*E*ver had the feeling that a mass of seaweed is engulfing your brain, body, heart, and spirit? That no matter how hard you try to get loose, things, people, events just keep pulling you down, down, down to the depths of despair? That you can't escape the mouth of the giant whale sucking you into its belly and the consuming darkness soon to follow?

First the washer breaks. Then the dryer. Your car gets a flat tire. Your phone dies. The kids need to be picked up. A document delivered. Dinner cooked. You are being pulled in so many different directions. If one more person asks you for a drink of water, a report that was due yesterday, or some spectacular wonder-woman feat from you, you just might explode.

Don't despair. Go to prayer. On your knees. If not physically, then mentally. But get there. For prayer is not your last resort but your first resource. Tapping into the power of God and your faith can draw you out of the darkness and into the light.

No matter how big or little your concerns, a caring God wants to hear from you and pull you up, giving you the strength and energy to meet the demands of this day only. Not yesterday, not tomorrow. But today. In whatever moment you find yourself. No matter who or what stands before you.

Go to your Father God and ask for whatever you need. Then expect that something good—strength, patience, peace, knowledge, inspiration—will be given to you. Because Jesus says, "If you then, evil as you are, know how to give good and advantageous gifts to your children, how much more will your Father Who is in heaven [perfect as He is] give good and advantageous things to those who keep on asking Him!" (Matthew 7:11 AMPC).

So go. Ask. And believe God will give you a great gift, a way to meet the demands before you. While you're at it, check in with Him. Find out if you're going down the road He wants you on. Or if you need to turn around, maybe take some things off your plate so you can live the life He's planned for you.

Don't despair. Go to prayer.

I'm so consumed by the wants and needs of others, Lord, that I don't even know what to ask for sometimes. I'm coming to You on my knees, Jesus, asking You to give me whatever I need to rise up out of the depth of my despair into the height of Your light. In Your name I pray.

Heart Treasure: In Jesus, I find the light.

Finding Your Way

Next Paul and Silas traveled through the area of Phrygia and Galatia,
because the Holy Spirit had prevented them from preaching the word
in the province of Asia at that time. Then coming to the borders of Mysia,
they headed north for the province of Bithynia, but again
the Spirit of Jesus did not allow them to go there.

ACTS 16:6–7 NLT

Some life-altering decisions are unfolding before you. *Is this the man I should marry? Is it time for another baby? Should I take this new position? Is it feasible to start taking retirement benefits now? When should I start this new ministry?*

You ask God. You speak to friends, consult experts, talk to family members, have a long chat with your boyfriend or husband, peruse self-help books, meet with your pastor. You get lots of advice. Then you ask God again. But you're not sure of His response. You feel you're not getting any clear direction.

So you dive into the Word, looking for guidance there. Maybe you read of David asking God if he should fight the Philistines. Of God's response, "Yes, go ahead" (1 Chronicles 14:10 NLT). Of how David then met with success! Of how when the Philistines returned, David went to God again with questions. This time, the Lord was even more specific with details of how to handle the dilemma, ending with "Go out. . .for God has gone out before you" (1 Chronicles 14:15 ESV). As a result of listening to and obeying God's advice, David met with success *again*. You begin thinking, *Why can't God answer me like that? I want the particulars! Where are You, Lord?*

Not getting a specific response from God, you do nothing. You stay planted where you are amid indecision and uncertainty. But that's not where God would have you be.

Continue asking God for direction, but be assured that He has not left you. He just hasn't yet made His will known—or you have not yet heard it. Either way, He's got His eye on you. If you feel the Spirit wants you to wait, be patient. Leave the issue in God's hands, knowing He knows best. If you decide to step out and end up making a wrong turn, know that the Spirit will redirect you. It happened for Paul and Silas. It can happen for you.

Jesus, my Lord and Savior, You know the big decisions that are before me. I truly don't know which way to turn. And I'm not sure what You want me to do. Please, Lord, give me some definite direction. Tell me which way to go. And if the way is still unclear, help me take the first steps, knowing Your Spirit will redirect me when and where needed. Amen.

Heart Treasure: In Jesus, I find my way.

....

....

....

....

....

....

....

....

....

....

....

....

....

....

....

Finding Your Wings

"So don't worry and don't keep saying, 'What shall we eat, what shall we drink or what shall we wear?' That is what pagans are always looking for; your Heavenly Father knows that you need them all. Set your heart on the kingdom and his goodness, and all these things will come to you as a matter of course."

MATTHEW 6:31–33 PHILLIPS

*Y*ou wake up in the morning, say a little prayer, perhaps read a devotion or two. You're filled with peace, calm, and great expectations. You sigh—happy, contented, carefree. And then your feet hit the floor. You shower and begin thinking of the day ahead, wondering how you'll get everything done. Then you go to your closet. *What to wear today? Hmm. Not that outfit. Too worn. Not that one. Doesn't fit anymore.* You sigh, this time in resignation, as you grab an outfit and say to yourself, "I guess this one will do."

You dress. Then meet the other household members, whether they be the cat, dog, husband, kids, or grandkids. They have a thousand questions of their own for you. "Did you get the paper?" "Can you pick me up from school?" "What do we have for breakfast?"

Suddenly you've lost your peace, calm, and great expectations. You begin to worry about the timing of all that lies before you—and not just today. The future begins creeping in. You wonder and worry about the week ahead, your thoughts launching into the weekend.

As you begin rinsing the breakfast dishes, you look out your kitchen window and see the birds hopping from branch to branch. You hear their sweet song and almost resentfully wonder how they can be so happy. As they sip the water from the birdbath, you see their beaks raised up to heaven, as if in thanks to God for what He's provided.

That's when it hits you. You remember the verse about the birds. "Look at the birds. They don't plant or harvest or store food in barns, for your heavenly Father feeds them. And aren't you far more valuable to him than they are?" (Matthew 6:26 NLT).

You stop. Your hands hang still in the air, suds dripping down. You hear Jesus' whisper, *"Don't worry. I've got you covered."* You smile. Content.

Next thing you know, you're singing.

Lord Jesus, thank You for taking such good care of me, for providing all I need. For reminding me that I need not worry. You have me covered. I put myself, my cares, my life, my loved ones into Your gentle hands. And as I do so, the song of joy You've planted in my heart takes flight. Amen.

Heart Treasure: In Jesus, I find my wings.

Finding the Right Perspective

Blessed (happy, enviably fortunate, and spiritually prosperous—possessing the happiness produced by the experience of God's favor and especially conditioned by the revelation of His grace, regardless of their outward conditions) are the pure in heart, for they shall see God!
MATTHEW 5:8 AMPC

*Y*ou're a regular churchgoer. You tithe each week. You may even have a ministry you love to be involved in. Yet when you look around at the rich, the famous, the ones who don't seem to have a care in this world, you start to wonder, *What about me, Lord? I play by the rules, do all the right things. But I find myself struggling to make ends meet. What's up with that? When will this life get easier?*

That's when your perspective has taken you out of the God zone. And it's not unusual to go there some days. The same thoughts have careened around human minds for thousands of years. Just ask Asaph, the author of Psalm 73. Although he knew God was good to the "pure in heart" (Psalm 73:1 AMPC), he nearly missed seeing His goodness because his eyes were "looking up to the people at the top, envying the wicked who have it made, who have nothing to worry about, not a care" (Psalm 73:3–5 MSG). He goes on and on about how he's had bad luck while the ungodly seem to prosper. When he tried to understand the disparity between the godly and the ungodly, he got a migraine for his efforts. He couldn't wrap his head around it.

But then the aching psalmist found his "until." And he found it in God's house. He writes, ". . .until I entered the sanctuary of God. Then I saw the whole picture: the slippery road you've put them on, with a final crash in a ditch of delusions" (Psalm 73:17–18 MSG).

When you're at the same crisis point, going down the same road of wondering why you seem to have so much less than those who don't follow the same rules—the ones God has set out for you to follow—go to

Jesus. Get so much of Him that you find His perspective. He has already told you that you'll be happier and more spiritually rich—no matter what your outward circumstances or conditions—when you are pure in heart. As *The Message* puts it, "You're blessed when you get your inside world—your mind and heart—put right. Then you can see God in the outside world" (Matthew 5:8).

Lord, I thank You for being with me. For turning my mind around to Your perspective. In You I have all the happiness and prosperity I could ever want. You make my mind and heart right, enabling me to see all the blessings of God surrounding me. Thank You for all this and more. Amen.

Heart Treasure: In Jesus, I find the right perspective.

Finding a Fixed Tent of Comfort

And the Word (Christ) became flesh (human, incarnate) and tabernacled (fixed His tent of flesh, lived awhile) among us; and we [actually] saw His glory (His honor, His majesty), such glory as an only begotten son receives from his father, full of grace (favor, loving-kindness) and truth.

JOHN 1:14 AMPC

*T*he book of John tells us that Jesus dwelled among us. The literal meaning of this is that He "pitched His tent." If you're not a camper, you may never have pitched a tent yourself. But it's likely you know the basics of the procedure anyway. Pegs are involved, along with poles or stakes, perhaps a ground cloth, and a mallet or rock.

According to the Online Etymology Dictionary, the etymological definition of the word *pitch* is "to thrust in, fasten, settle." When you pitch your tent, you've thrust in the pegs, fastened down the tent, settled it into the earth.

In the Old Testament, a lot of tent pitching was going on. The patriarchs Abraham, Isaac, and Jacob pitched tents over and over again (Genesis 12:8; 26:17, 25). Even Moses pitched a tent (Exodus 33:7), as did the Israelites in the wilderness (Numbers 1:52). God even directed the tent pitchers; Moses told the people that God "went in the way before you to search out a place to pitch your tents, in fire by night, to show you by what way you should go, and in the cloud by day" (Deuteronomy 1:33 AMPC).

So why all this talk about pitching tents? To remind you that during times of confusion, lack of direction, loneliness, doubt, and desperation, you need not panic or despair. All you need to do is remember and believe that Jesus came and pitched His tent—physically. And that when you began to believe in Him, He pitched His tent over you, in you, around you—spiritually. Jesus not only dwelled among God's children to show them the way, the truth, the light; He became one of us. He lived, breathed, wept, walked, and loved in the wilderness of life, just as we live, breathe, weep, walk, and love in the wilderness of our own lives. As a result, He knows just what you're going through and so can comfort you like no other.

To go deeper into this idea, consider sitting back, closing your eyes, and imagining Jesus pitching His tent over you. Allow His light, love, and peace to cover you. Take in His comfort.

Thank You, Jesus, for dwelling within me, pitching Your tent of love and life, of peace and hope over me. Words cannot express the overwhelming comfort I feel because You are here, always with me, helping me find my way in the wilderness of this life. Help me settle into this fact and keep it with me throughout this moment, this day, this life. Amen.

Heart Treasure: In Jesus, I find a fixed tent of comfort.

....

....

....

....

....

....

....

....

....

....

....

....

....

....

Finding Healing Power

"Daughter, you took a risk trusting me, and now you're
healed and whole. Live well, live blessed!"
LUKE 8:48 MSG

*Y*ou're a woman. You have issues. Whether they be physical, mental, or spiritual, these issues are ongoing. You've seen all the doctors, the professionals. They've taken your money. But some of their remedies leave you either unchanged or worse off than before. You're about to accept this issue as your lot in life.

Such was the case of the woman who had an issue of blood. She'd been hemorrhaging for twelve years! The doctors had taken all her money. And then she heard that Jesus was going to be coming her way. She crept through the crowd, coming up behind the great Man. She reached out for Him. As she did so, she was saying to herself, "If I only touch his garment, I will be made well" (Matthew 9:21 ESV). And as soon as she "touched the fringe of his garment. . .immediately her discharge of blood ceased" (Luke 8:44 ESV).

At the same time the woman was healed, "Jesus, perceiving in himself that power had gone out from him, immediately turned about in the crowd" and asked who'd touched Him (Mark 5:30 ESV). Although the disciples responded that dozens of people had touched Him, Jesus "went on asking, looking around to see who had done it" (Mark 5:32 MSG).

Finally, the woman, fearful and trembling, fell at Jesus' feet, confessing that she had touched Him, had received His power, and was now whole again.

Jesus' response? "Daughter, you took a risk of faith, and now you're healed and whole. Live well, live blessed! Be healed of your plague" (Mark 5:34 MSG).

Three of the Gospels—Matthew, Mark, and Luke—contain this account.

Their reports may vary slightly, but the means to the end are the same. This woman who had suffered for years, who had exhausted all the wisdom of herself and the professionals, finally got it in her head to reach out to Jesus as He was passing by.

She disregarded the crowds. She persevered, finding her way through the throng of needy people. She kept saying to herself, "If I just reach out and touch Him, I'll be healed." She grasped the fringe of His garment, and Jesus' healing power surged through her, stopping her issue from being an issue. She took a risk of faith and was richly rewarded—made whole and addressed by the Master Healer Himself! He called her a daughter, commended her act of faith, then blessed her life!

Determine to reach out for Jesus, and you too will receive His healing power.

Lord Jesus, I'm pushing my way through the crowd to You. In faith I reach out to touch You—and to receive Your touch in return. May Your healing power surge through me. And as You make me whole, may I fall on my knees in thanks and praise.

Heart Treasure: In Jesus, I find healing power.

....

....

....

....

....

....

....

....

Finding Peace Suddenly

But quite suddenly, Jesus stood before them in their path, and said,
"Peace be with you!" And they went forward to meet him and, clasping his
feet, worshipped him. Then Jesus said to them, "Do not be afraid."
MATTHEW 28:9–10 PHILLIPS

*S*uddenly! Oh, how one can grow to dislike that word. For things in life often happen suddenly, and instant change sometimes makes us lose our balance.

Suddenly, you lose your temper. Suddenly, your husband is laid off. Suddenly, you hit a car—or a car hits you. Suddenly, your child has the flu and your well-planned day goes off the rails. Suddenly, suddenly, suddenly, something has happened and, as a result, your heart is in your throat, the unknown looms before you, and you're out of control.

Even the disciples were hit by a "suddenly," not just once but many times. Consider the account in Matthew 8:23–27. Jesus got into a boat. The disciples followed Him. "And suddenly, behold, there arose a violent storm on the sea, so that the boat was being covered up by the waves" (Matthew 8:24 AMPC). So what was Jesus doing? Sleeping the sleep of the faith-filled.

So the disciples woke Him up, crying, "Lord, Master! Rescue us! Save us! We're in big trouble, about to go down into the dark sea!"

Jesus calmly replied, "Why are you timid and afraid, O you of little faith?" (Matthew 8:26 AMPC). Hmm. Faith. The never-failing remedy for all "suddenlys."

"Then He got up and rebuked the winds and the sea, and there was a great and wonderful calm (a perfect peaceableness)" (Matthew 8:26 AMPC). The *sudden* calm left the disciples stunned and confused, filled with wonder. Even the seas and wind obeyed this Jesus.

So it seems not all "suddenly" events are bad. Remember when John baptized Jesus? "Suddenly the heavens opened and he saw the Spirit of God coming down" (Matthew 3:16 PHILLIPS). At Jesus' tomb, "suddenly the earth reeled and rocked under their feet as God's angel came down. . . . He rolled back the stone" (Matthew 28:2 MSG). And when Christ's female followers were hurrying away from the tomb to tell the disciples He had risen, "quite suddenly, Jesus stood before them in their path, and said, 'Peace be with you!' " (Matthew 28:9 PHILLIPS).

With Jesus there's no reason to fear when a "suddenly" appears in your life. For He has power over everything coming against you, making a "suddenly" seem not so bad after all. In fact, with Jesus, you'll find "*suddenly*" is a good thing—for His peace, glory, and strength are right behind.

Thank You, Lord, for always being there amid my storms, bringing Your calm into my life. Help me to keep Your presence in mind—and heart— when a "suddenly" is thrown my way. Remind me that You are standing in my path, suddenly bringing Your peace to me.

Heart Treasure: In Jesus, I find peace suddenly.

Seeking and Finding

Do not seek [by meditating and reasoning to inquire into] what you are to eat and what you are to drink; nor be of anxious (troubled) mind [unsettled, excited, worried, and in suspense]. . . . Only aim at and strive for and seek His kingdom, and all these things shall be supplied to you also.
LUKE 12:29, 31 AMPC

*W*omen usually have a plan. And not just for themselves, but for their loved ones. And that plan is to keep everyone safe, secure, on the "right" track, and, if possible, happy.

So we get a bit miffed, unsettled, worried when something disrupts those plans, whether the disruption be big or little. But there is a surefire way to quell those feelings of troubled suspense.

Jesus tells you to seek God and His kingdom. Then He'll supply everything you need. And not just food, clothing, and such. Not just the material goods. When you trust in and lean on God, checking in with Him at every step along the way, you'll find the peace that surpasses all understanding.

But that "seeking" is not just to be a quick once-a-day seeking of God. It's to be ongoing. As King David wrote, "Seek the Lord and His strength; yearn for and seek His face and to be in His presence *continually*!" (1 Chronicles 16:11 AMPC, emphasis added). The Message puts that verse and the one that follows like this: "Study GOD and his strength, seek his presence *day and night*; remember all the wonders he performed" (emphasis added).

"Continually." "Day and night." Are you doing such seeking? Are you also shoring up your faith in God and His strength by thinking back on all the amazing things He has done in your life?

When David wrote 1 Chronicles 16:11–12, he'd just had the ark of God brought into Jerusalem where he'd pitched a tent for God's presence. Those words were just the beginning of a thanksgiving song he had the Levites sing. Then he instructed them not just to seek God *day and night* but to "give thanks to the LORD, for his steadfast love endures forever" (1 Chronicles 16:41 ESV). After that, "David went home to bless his household" (verse 43 ESV).

You see, when you seek God, trusting in Him *continually*, thanking Him for what He has done, is doing, and will do, not only do your worries fade, but you find yourself blessing your household, those you love, those for whom God's plans stand firm—knowing *His* are the best plans of all.

You know the plans I have for myself and those I love, Lord. But I want to put seeking You, loving You, and following You first in my life. Help me to carry out Your good plans for me. Thank You, Lord, for Your love. Amen.

Heart Treasure: In Jesus, I seek and find.

Finding Your Mind and Heart

For as he thinks in his heart, so is he.
PROVERBS 23:7 AMPC

*W*here's my head today? Has that question ever entered your mind? Have you ever had your plate so full, and then had so many unexpected interruptions, that your plans went by the wayside, confusion settled in, and you lost your focus on the tasks at hand?

No worries. It happens to all of us. But when we start wondering where we may have lost our heads, perhaps it's also time to consider where our hearts are.

Today's verse says, "For as he thinks in his heart, so is he." Hmm. So as we think in our hearts, deep down, that's what we are. That's what comes out. But Jesus takes it further, saying, "For where your treasure is, there will your heart be also" (Matthew 6:21 AMPC). He follows that up with, "No one can serve two masters; for either he will hate the one and love the other, or he will stand by and be devoted to the one and despise and be against the other. You cannot serve God and mammon (deceitful riches, money, possessions, or whatever is trusted in)" (Matthew 6:24 AMPC).

That's a lot to take in. But all these ideas are pointing in the same direction.

As we go through our days, as we put our hands to our tasks, what are our thoughts? Where are our hearts? Do we do things grudgingly or lovingly?

What are our hearts set upon? Furthering the kingdom of God by doing things in love, no matter how arduous or how ungrateful the recipients of our efforts? Are our hearts trusting in God or in the things we can gain by our labor? Who are we really serving—God, ourselves, the "almighty dollar," or the world around us?

It's time to get head-smart and heart-smart. To renew our minds before, during, and after a task. To remember who we're doing it for, the One in whom our treasure really lies—Jesus.

But how do we do that? In the morning, give the day and all the tasks that may fall into your hands into God's keeping. No matter what comes against you, keep in your mind and heart the reason you're doing what you're doing. Relax knowing God is in charge of the results of all your efforts. He'll work everything out for the good—for His good.

Where is your heart today? Where are your thoughts? Be sure they are centered on Jesus.

I feel so scattered sometimes, Lord. And in those moments, it's almost as if I'm trying to make my way through a fog. Help me to keep my heart and thoughts centered on You, Jesus. To do everything with Your heart of love, with my thoughts and goals aimed toward extending Your kingdom. May You alone be my true treasure.

Heart Treasure: In Jesus, I find my mind and heart.

Finding the Blessings of Giving

In everything I have pointed out to you [by example] that, by working diligently in this manner, we ought to assist the weak, being mindful of the words of the Lord Jesus, how He Himself said, It is more blessed (makes one happier and more to be envied) to give than to receive.

ACTS 20:35 AMPC

*Y*ou had an idea of what your day would look like, what things you'd get done. In spite of all the interruptions, you managed to cross a few things off your list. You have just enough time to pick up a prescription for your mom who's not able to get out and about anymore. Or just enough time to get dinner ready. Or just enough time to get that one last thing done. And then you get a phone call from church, a text message from a friend, or an email from a coworker, or perhaps you just hear, "Hey, Mom!" or "Hey, honey!" or "Hey, [insert your name here]!" Any one or all of these end up with some request taking the last ounce of your strength, courage, and patience—none of which you feel you can spare. But then, through gritted teeth, you agree to take on this new, unexpected errand, chore, task.

At first your head is in the wrong place. So's your heart. You hardly ever get a thank-you for all you do. Your thoughts grow darker. *How can people expect so much of me? I'm not Superwoman.* Your feet become like lead, though you keep walking forward. And then as you begin to perform this new errand, you find your energy coming back. Suddenly you have feet like a deer, able to climb to new heights. Your heart becomes lighter as well as your thoughts. You get a smile, a thank-you. And you suddenly realize it was worth all your time, trouble, and effort.

The apostle Paul addressed some very wise words to his fellow Christ followers. Before going off on his next arduous mission, he reminded them where they got their power: "Now I'm turning you over to God, our marvelous God whose gracious Word can make you into what he wants you to be and give you everything you could possibly need" (Acts 20:32 MSG). And he reminded them of the blessings of doing what they were called to do: "You'll not likely go wrong here if you keep remembering that our Master said, 'You're far happier giving than getting' " (Acts 20:35 MSG).

Lord Jesus, You are my strength and energy. You know how much better it is to give than to receive. Please help me to keep this truth in mind— and heart—as I go through my day. Help me to realize that a thanks from You is all the blessing I need and the one I am sure to receive.

Heart Treasure: In Jesus, I find the blessings of giving.

Finding Rest and Sleep

The apostles then rendezvoused with Jesus and reported on all that they had done and taught. Jesus said, "Come off by yourselves; let's take a break and get a little rest."
MARK 6:30–31 MSG

Ever have those nights when you just can't get any sleep? Thoughts are careening around in your head. The what-ifs and how-comes, the would'ves, should'ves, and could'ves are keeping your eyes from shutting. You almost feel like you might as well get up again, maybe put your hand to some knitting, read a book, or grab a snack, perhaps try to swallow some warm milk. Before going that route, why not lean into the Word?

After the apostles had been out and about, they were obviously exhausted. So much so that Jesus told them to come with Him to a quiet place and get some rest for a while. In human form, Jesus knew that rest for Himself and His followers was a means of renewal so that they could continue to do what they'd been called to do.

If you seek, you will find lots of treasures, reassuring verses in the Old Testament to help you get some much-needed shut-eye. Here are a few to sink into:

- "First pay attention to me, and then relax. Now you can take it easy—you're in good hands" (Proverbs 1:33 MSG).
- "Relax and rest. GOD has showered you with blessings" (Psalm 116:7 MSG).
- "Sit back and relax, my dear daughter, until we find out how things turn out" (Ruth 3:18 MSG).

Try looking up some verses of your own, ones that speak directly to your heart in this time and place. Many scriptures are not just about rest but about actual sleep, such as these:

- "I lay down and slept, yet I woke up in safety, for the LORD was watching over me" (Psalm 3:5 NLT).

- "In peace I will lie down and sleep, for you alone, O LORD, will keep me safe" (Psalm 4:8 NLT).

And take to heart this verse that reminds you that even as you sleep, all is well:

"He will not let you stumble; the one who watches over you will not slumber. Indeed, he who watches over Israel never slumbers or sleeps" (Psalm 121:3–4 NLT).

Know that the King of kings, the Lord of lords is waiting to give you rest and refreshment. That you can rest secure in your Good Shepherd's arms. He's guarding the gate to your heart and mind, making sure no wolves can creep in. Rest assured of His watchful care for the entire you—heart, mind, body, spirit, and soul.

Lord, guide me to the verses, the thoughts I need to get the sleep my body craves. Impress them upon me so that I can lean back into You, assured that while I sleep, all is well.

Heart Treasure: In Jesus, I find rest and sleep.

....

....

....

....

....

....

....

....

....

Finding Perseverance in Prayer

And he told them a parable to the effect that they
ought always to pray and not lose heart.
LUKE 18:1 ESV

*H*ave you ever felt as if your prayers to God are going unanswered? Have you lost hope about a certain situation, thinking God may not even be listening anymore?

Perhaps you've been praying for a family member to be saved, to realize God is a very real Person who wants to come into their life. But so far, they've shown no sign of even coming close to God. Maybe you've been praying about where your next meal will come from and are still wondering about it day after day. Perhaps you've been praying about and wondering if you'll ever get paid as much as your male counterpart. It may be that you have a heart for someone (perhaps yourself) who's being persecuted for her faith, yet you feel God hasn't heard your prayers because her situation remains unchanged.

Take heart. God does hear your prayers. Jesus tells you not to give up. Then He relates the parable of the persistent widow.

Here's a woman probably rated the lowest of the low because she has no male to represent her in her patriarchal society. She goes before an unjust judge who has no time for God, asking him to help her against her adversary. For a long time the judge refuses to help her cause. And then finally, tired of her constant pleading, the judge gives in and rules in her favor because "she is wearing me out with her constant requests!" (Luke 18:5 NLT).

Jesus' point is that if an unjust judge who doesn't even know or respect God finally steps in to help this poor widow, for whom he cares nothing, "what makes you think God won't step in and work justice for his chosen people, who continue to cry out for help? Won't he stick up for them?

I assure you, he will" (Luke 18:7–8 MSG). For your God is an amazingly compassionate God who loves, cares for, and wants the best for you.

"But when?" you might ask. "When will I see the answer to my prayers?"

In God's time. He has a plan for your life and the lives of those you love. He has everything under control. Trust that truth; realize it as a fact.

In the meantime, don't lose heart. Keep bringing your requests before God, knowing that He does hear you and is working things out. Then let the peace of that knowledge sink into your mind and buoy your heart.

Lord, thank You for always listening to me, for caring for me, for wanting the best for me and mine. Help me to continue to persevere in prayer. To have the faith and trust that You are indeed working things out. In Jesus' name I pray, amen.

Heart Treasure: In Jesus, I find I can persevere in prayer.

Finding Solace

*J*t's okay. Everything will be all right."

Have you ever heard those words from your mom or dad, a good friend, your husband, someone who loves you like no other? As soon as someone tells you it's going to be all right, an amazing thing happens. You release a breath you didn't realize you were holding. Your heart settles. The worries about when your house will sell, when you'll get that new job, when you'll find out the test results. . .all those things you're fretting about don't seem so weighty.

But when you hear those words from Jesus, when you hear Him say, "Don't let this throw you. You trust God, don't you? Trust me" (John 14:1 MSG), when you remember He's your rock and your refuge, that's when you realize everything really *is* fine.

Second Kings 4:8–37 tells of a Shunammite woman who had a husband and wealth but no children. When the prophet Elisha passed her way, she'd invite him in for food. Knowing him to be a man of God, she, with the approval of her husband, makes a small room for him. Elisha, wanting to do something kind for her in return, asks what he can do for her. A contented woman, she asks for nothing. Yet the prophet, burning to do something nice for her, tells her she'll bear a son next year. And she does.

The boy grows. Then one day, quite suddenly, he has a pain in his head. He's put on his mother's lap and later dies in her arms. She carries her son up to Elisha's room and places him on the prophet's bed. Then she determines to find Elisha. When her husband questions her about where she's going, she merely responds with, "It will be all right" (2 Kings 4:23 NLT).

Elisha's servant Gehazi sees her coming out to meet them. He runs to meet her, asking if all is well. She responds, "Everything is fine" (2 Kings 4:26 NLT), for Gehazi is not the one she is hurrying to meet. Finally, she reaches Elisha and explains the situation, and her son is brought back to life.

What faith this woman had! What contentment. When trouble came, she knew who to run to—a man of God. And while on the run, her faith enabled her to tell others, "It's okay. Everything will be all right." And in the end, it was, according to God's will.

Cling to the safety net of Jesus. Know that with Him, no matter what happens, all will be all right. Trust in Him, rely on His Word, believe in Him—and also in God.

I'm running to You, Lord. Allow Your comforting words—
"It's okay"—to permeate my entire being as I trust in You,
Jesus, for everything. In You, I find all the comfort I need.

Heart Treasure: In Jesus, I find solace.

Finding the Illuminating Truth

*I have still many things to say to you, but you are not able to bear
them or to take them upon you or to grasp them now. But when He,
the Spirit of Truth (the Truth-giving Spirit) comes, He will guide
you into all the Truth (the whole, full Truth).*

JOHN 16:12–13 AMPC

It's that time of day. The same time most every day that you sigh and
sit down to read your devotional or the next Bible chapters in your
reading plan. Or it's the usual Sunday school class, the usual topic. You
pull the student book from your bag and open it to today's lesson. Or you
open up the Bible to the passage the pastor has selected to preach on.

You're not really expecting anything. Your mind is focused on what's
coming up in the day ahead, but your hands know the routine as you open
the book, turn the pages, and prepare to read, to hear, to study.

Then all of a sudden, you stop in your tracks. It's almost as if a light
has come down from heaven and illuminated the page. Words jump out at
you. You find the answer to a question you didn't even know you had! Or
you see the solution to a problem you thought unsolvable. Or you discover
a new path, a new way, something that gives you just the direction you
need. The words of Psalm 119:105 (MSG) echo in your brain: "By your words
I can see where I'm going; they throw a beam of light on my dark path."

In the midst of your routine, God has spoken. The things you could
not hear before, the truths you weren't ready to grasp until now, suddenly
make all the sense in the world. That's the Holy Spirit working in your
midst, guiding you into the truth of Jesus' Word!

The Word is never routine. It's always opening new doors, giving you
a new perspective in your life. No matter your condition, preconceptions,
or attitude, God's Word can and will blow your mind.

Make it your intent to approach God's Word with curiosity. Believe
that just what you need—whether you know it yet or not—is waiting to

be revealed. Be like the miner looking for that nugget of gold. Before you open the Book, open your mind, ears, spirit, and heart. Ask the Holy Spirit to guide you into the whole truth—and nothing but the truth—that He wants to show you, that is ready to be revealed. Make your seeking of God a blessed adventure.

Jesus, I'm here before You, ready, willing, and able to hear Your voice speak to me. Illuminate the concepts You're ready to reveal to me. Help me to carry them with me throughout my day, to incorporate them into my life. I'm here, listening, ready for the blessed adventure.

Heart Treasure: In Jesus, I find the illuminating truth.

....

....

....

....

....

....

....

....

....

....

....

....

....

Finding Joy

*"When a woman gives birth, she has a hard time, there's no getting
around it. But when the baby is born, there is joy in the birth.
This new life in the world wipes out memory of the pain."*
JOHN 16:21 MSG

*J*t's true—"there's no getting around it." There will be times of trial,
sorrow, pain, and anguish in this life. Jesus says so.

And it's amazing that Jesus, this Man, uses childbirth to illustrate to
the male disciples the suffering they'll encounter.

Many of us may remember the pain we suffered while giving birth—and
the difficulties encountered during pregnancy. The feeling that something
foreign has invaded our body, taken us over. The morning sickness, the
heaviness, the pressing of the baby's weight on our bladder. The not being
able to see our feet at some point, nor being able to get up out of a chair.

After all that, just when we think we can't take it anymore, the
contractions start. And even though we've done all we can to prepare
ourselves for the "blessed event," nothing we've read, watched, or heard
compares to the reality of the mess, indignity, and pain. As comedian
Carol Burnett says, "Giving birth is like taking your lower lip and forcing
it over your head."

Yet afterward—once the pain is over, we're stitched back together,
and a clean sheet is put on the bed—if all goes well, we get this precious
life, for which we are now responsible, put into our arms. And the joy is
incomparable. Soon all the memories of what we've gone through are
practically erased. (Otherwise, we'd never have child number two!)

Jesus' point is that, yes, we will have times of hardship. We will suffer
loss, grief, and anguish. But we need not fear, for Jesus is near. Once the
pain is over, He stitches us back up. He cleans everything up. He places
joy we never even thought possible into our arms. And all the pain we've

56

suffered dims in the light of the happiness we have in Him.

Jesus says, "So also you have sorrow now, but I will see you again, and your hearts will rejoice, and no one will take your joy from you" (John 16:22 ESV). Keep that truth close to your heart and mind. Allow it to fill your spirit. Know that no matter what you're facing or have faced, Jesus holds all the joy you could ever want or imagine.

Lord Jesus, I'm amazed You know me so intimately. And I'm thrilled at the thought, the truth, that no matter what I'm going through now, You're waiting at the end of it with an armful of joy that no one will be able to take from me. Thank You for all that You have done, are doing, and will do in my life to bring me that unsurpassable, unearthly joy.

Heart Treasure: In Jesus, I find joy.

Finding the Right Words

"A good person produces good things from the treasury of a good heart, and an evil person produces evil things from the treasury of an evil heart. What you say flows from what is in your heart."

LUKE 6:45 NLT

*Y*ikes! It's happened again! The words I shouldn't have said just flowed right out of my mouth and ended up slapping someone else in the face!

Your tongue, the words you say, can reveal a lot about you. Jesus says that what you say reveals to others what's truly in your heart.

That's a hard truth to swallow. Our tongues get in the way.

Jesus said these words from Luke 6:45 just after He'd told His listeners not to judge others. To take the plank out of their own eyes before trying to remove the toothpick from the eyes of others.

Perhaps your words are tinged with the words your parents, teachers, or so-called friends once said to you. Words repeated often enough to us become the thoughts we think about ourselves and others. Perhaps someone once (twice, three times, or more) told you that you weren't good enough, smart enough, pretty enough, rich enough, ambitious enough, stylish enough. And now that idea is planted not just in your mind but in your heart. Perhaps you feel compelled to tell others the same thing. God forbid!

So how do you get a heart full of good treasure? You allow the heavenly love of God and Jesus to reign in your heart. Such a stock will allow you to spend that love by speaking it over others. You'll find yourself building them up instead of tearing them down.

While you're speaking good over others, consider monitoring your own thoughts, the ones you speak to yourself, holding them captive to Christ (2 Corinthians 10:5). Allow His love to erase the echoes of *You're not good enough*. Replace them with the heart knowledge that your name is engraved on the palms of God's hands (Isaiah 49:16). You're precious to God; in fact, He honors and loves you (Isaiah 43:4). God loved you so much that He allowed His one and only Son to die in your place (John 3:16)!

Store up all these truths, all these treasures, in your heart. Speak good words, God's good words, over yourself and into the lives of others. When you slip up (and chances are you will), ask God and those you may have wounded (including yourself) for forgiveness. And determine to do better, with God's help and love.

Fill me with Your presence and Your love, Jesus. Give me the words and thoughts You want me to have, those that build up myself and others. And when my mouth careens out of control, help me to quickly right the wrong. Be my Word—in speech and deed. In Your name I pray, amen.

Heart Treasure: In Jesus, I find the right words.

Finding Security

*And I will ask the Father, and He will give you another Comforter
(Counselor, Helper, Intercessor, Advocate, Strengthener,
and Standby), that He may remain with you forever.*
JOHN 14:16 AMPC

ome days you feel a need to find some time to be alone. You're a bit
down but not really sure why. Perhaps it's the world's woes. Or maybe
you're exhausted and need to recharge before you say or do something
you'll be sorry for. Or you've just suffered some kind of heartache and
need a good cry.

No matter the cause, you need to hunker down until this nameless
storm passes over you. So you sneak off into a quiet room, put on a
treasured movie, and ease down into your favorite chair. Or you put on
some soothing music, pick up your yarn and needles, and zone out for an
afternoon, just you and the wool sliding through your fingers. Or you go
for a walk, taking in the beauty of nature around you. Or you pick up a
book and lose yourself within its pages, away from the reality around you
and into someone else's world that soon becomes your own.

Yes, we all need our downtime. A chance to escape this world, to
get away from our problems, obligations, commitments, and to-dos. An
opportunity to refill and refuel.

Yet when we take this time to just be, to "find ourselves again," we
should also take the opportunity to reach out to the Comforter. You
know, the one Jesus sent—the Holy Spirit. Because we're women of the
Way, believers and receivers of Christ, the Holy Spirit is here to help us
in whatever way we need. He's on standby for when we need to fall back
into helping arms, to be lifted up so we can once again face the world—and
its people—around us.

That spiritual Comforter is just the warm, cozy blanket we need to wrap up in. When we do, we can't help but feel His strength all around us. In His presence, we realize we're never really alone. We have Him to remain with us forever, to take the place of Jesus in physical form.

In those moments when you're ready to retreat to that solitary place and get replenished, reach out to the Holy Spirit before you reach for the movie, music, yarn, book, or knob on the door. Take a moment to breathe Him in. Allow the Holy Spirit, the Comforter, to be the security blanket you cling to throughout your life.

Jesus, thank You for sending the Holy Spirit—my Standby, my Comforter— to my side, into my life. As I breathe Him in, I feel His strength wrap around me, securing me in this life. I'm clinging to You, Lord, everywhere I go, knowing You're the one who renews me.

Heart Treasure: In Jesus, I find security.

Finding Your Needs Met

"Give us this day our daily bread."
MATTHEW 6:11 ESV

*A*sking God to give us the bread we need today seems like a good idea, a simple concept, one we can easily grasp. It comes tripping off our tongues when we say the Lord's Prayer. It's a phrase we've memorized. But have we taken its words, especially *daily*, to heart?

It's easy to be in the "now" when we first wake up each day. We open our eyes. Then as we close them again, figuring we'll get in a couple extra z's, our brains do an automatic check-in with the body. *Am I cold? Do I have to go to the bathroom? Am I hungry?* All these are "now" questions. Yet they soon morph into future thoughts. *I'm hungry for a muffin. If I eat that last one today, what will I eat tomorrow?*

See? We're already there! In the future. Didn't take long, did it?

The point is, God wants us to be focused more on trusting Him for what we need in the moment, *for that day*, than on thinking about what we may need in the future.

Proverbs 30:8–9 (ESV) gives us more insight into the daily-bread concept: "Give me neither poverty nor riches; feed me with the food that is needful for me, lest I be full and deny you and say, 'Who is the LORD?' or lest I be poor and steal and profane the name of my God." Those verses are telling us that we can trust God to give us just what we need—no more, no less. That definitely gives us a lot to chew on.

Remember the Israelites in the wilderness? God rained down just enough manna for them to eat that day. Any extra they gathered (in their attempt to store up against future need) just ended up rotting, becoming worm infested. Of course, on the sixth day of their week, God gave them twice as much so they wouldn't have to gather manna the next day, the Sabbath, their day of rest (Exodus 16:23).

The idea is to receive what God has provided for you *today*. And to do so with a grateful heart, not worry over what He may or may not provide tomorrow. When you do, you'll find yourself less anxious and more in the now, trusting God with a full heart—and belly.

I trust You, God, to provide just what I need just when I need it. In doing so, I feel my worries melt away and I grow closer and closer to You. Thank You, Jesus, for blessing me each and every moment as You give me this day my daily bread. In Your name I pray, amen.

Heart Treasure: In Jesus, I find my daily needs met.

Finding Courage to Be a Blessing

"Don't be bluffed into silence by the threats of bullies.
There's nothing they can do to your soul, your core being."
MATTHEW 10:28 MSG

God has a plan for your life. And He made you just who you are, a special person with a unique personality, history, experiences, and talents. He made you that way so you could accomplish what He wants you to do to bless the lives of others.

Yet you may find yourself hesitating to do what God has called you to do. Perhaps the naysayers around you, the discouragers, the belittlers, have planted seeds of doubt in your mind. Maybe someone has told you that you aren't good enough. Or worse, you've grown to believe it yourself. Or maybe the world situation has you so focused on what's happening around you that you're afraid to move forward, your hands lax at your sides. But Jesus has a message for you. *Go! Don't. . .be. . .afraid.*

Along with His power, Jesus sent out the twelve disciples with a lot of instructions, including that they were not to fear their fellow human beings! And He's sending you out the same way!

If you still have doubts, go to Jesus in prayer. Tell Him exactly what you're thinking, what you're fearing. Allow His presence to wash over you, filling you with all the power you need to do what He has called you to do.

Seek Jesus' voice through God's Word. Ask the Holy Spirit to guide you. Take up and claim the verses that speak to your heart. Hear God's voice telling you:

- "You shall be a blessing. Fear not, but let your hands be strong" (Zechariah 8:13 AMPC).
- "Don't be afraid, for I am with you. Don't be discouraged, for I am your God. I will strengthen you and help you. I will hold you up with my victorious right hand" (Isaiah 41:10 NLT).

Use the words of the Psalms to see God's commands for you—to not fear, to know that He is with you and will deliver you—in a more personal light:

- "The LORD is on my side; I will not fear. What can man do to me? The LORD is on my side as my helper" (Psalm 118:6–7 ESV).
- "I prayed to the LORD, and he answered me. He freed me from all my fears. Those who look to him for help will be radiant with joy; no shadow of shame will darken their faces" (Psalm 34:4–5 NLT).

Just as Jesus is an answer to your prayer, *you* are the answer to His. So go with God. Do not fear. Lift your hands and be a blessing.

Lord Jesus, with You by my side, I fear nothing. Give strength to my hands to do what You have called me to do. I want to be a blessing in Your name. Amen.

Heart Treasure: In Jesus, I find the courage to be a blessing.

Finding Your Way to Jesus' Side

"Go on your way then," returned Jesus, "your faith has healed you."
And he recovered his sight at once and followed Jesus along the road.
MARK 10:52 PHILLIPS

You've been going along, doing all that's in your strength and power to do, and still things don't seem to be meshing. You're at the end of your patience. Not sure what to do next, you cry out to Jesus. Good decision.

That's what the blind man Bartimeus did. As Jesus and His followers were heading out of Jericho, Bartimeus was sitting on the side of the road. When he heard that Jesus was passing through, he cried out, "Jesus, Son of David, have pity on me!" (Mark 10:47 PHILLIPS). When people tried to shush him, he cried out even louder: "Son of David, have pity on me!" (Mark 10:48 PHILLIPS).

And that's when Jesus stopped in His tracks. In fact, "Jesus stood quite still" (Mark 10:49 PHILLIPS). Then He told the disciples to call Bartimeus over. That's when the ones who had been discouraging him from coming to Jesus now encouraged him to do so, saying, "It's all right now, get up, he's calling you!" (Mark 10:49 PHILLIPS).

Hearing this good news, Bartimeus threw his coat aside, jumped up from the road, and ran to Jesus' side. Jesus responded to the blind man's arrival by asking him a simple question: "What do you want me to do for you?" (Mark 10:51 PHILLIPS). Most likely, Jesus was giving Bartimeus a chance to express his trust in Him. And he did, saying, "Oh, Master, let me see again!" (Mark 10:51 PHILLIPS). At the same time that Jesus responded to the blind man's prayer, saying, "Go on your way then. . .your faith has healed you" (Mark 10:52 PHILLIPS), the man was healed!

Know that you can't do everything in your own power. That your prayers for help are not an interruption but an invitation for Jesus to do something in your life. That you need to throw aside all that may hinder when you run to Him. That you can exchange the roadside for Jesus' side. All He's waiting for is for you to put your request into words. For doing so not only helps you to make clear your desire—to yourself and the Master—but shows you have trust in Him and His power. Then you'll find your way, your prayer answered, your sight restored.

And when it's all said and done, remember to continue to trust and follow Jesus down the road, staying in the wake of His power and blessing.

I'm coming to You, Lord, throwing off all that could hinder and running from the roadside of my way to that of Your Way. I'm asking for _____, knowing that my faith in You will clear my path as I continue to follow in Your wake. Thank You, Lord, for Your answer to my need. Amen.

Heart Treasure: In Jesus, I find my way to His side.

Finding God's Kingdom

"If you want to give it all you've got," Jesus replied, "go sell your
possessions; give everything to the poor. All your wealth will then be in
heaven. Then come follow me." That was the last thing the young man
expected to hear. And so, crestfallen, he walked away. He was holding
on tight to a lot of things, and he couldn't bear to let go.
MATTHEW 19:21–22 MSG

A rich young ruler asked Jesus what he needed to do to have eternal
life. Jesus told him to follow the Ten Commandments. When the
young man said, "I've done all that. What's left?" (Matthew 19:20 MSG),
Jesus said he should give all he had to the poor then follow Him. But the
man couldn't do it. He had too firm a grip on the things he'd already
accumulated.

What's keeping you from the kingdom of heaven? What are you
holding on to so tightly that you're having trouble releasing all to Jesus,
leaving all to follow Him?

It doesn't have to be money. It can be any other material possession
you may have. Or perhaps it's an intangible thing. Maybe you're too
self-reliant. You were raised to fend for yourself. To support and look out
for yourself. So why look to Jesus for help? You don't need to bother Him
with every little issue.

But that's not the attitude or mind-set that Jesus wants you to have.
For when you cling to self-reliance, you're limiting what He can do in
your life.

When Jesus told the disciples that it's more possible for a camel to fit
through the eye of a needle than for a rich man to enter God's kingdom,
the disciples were blown away. So they asked Jesus, "Then who has any
chance at all?" (Matthew 19:25 MSG). "Jesus looked hard at them and said,
'No chance at all if you think you can pull it off yourself. Every chance in
the world if you trust God to do it' " (Matthew 19:26 MSG).

Hmm. That gives a woman with a self-sufficient attitude something to think about.

Consider letting go of a few things, little by little, and putting them into Jesus' hands. Start with the small things. Then continue on, relying more and more on Him until your hands are fully open and ready to receive all of His help, not just bits and pieces here and there. When you do, you'll be amazed at how much your faith, trust, peace, and joy have grown.

Help me, Lord, to open my hands and let go of all that keeps me from trusting in You. I want to give up my all for You. Show me how to release what stands between You and me, Jesus. Help my self-reliance to diminish as my faith in You grows. Amen.

Heart Treasure: In Jesus, I find God's kingdom.

Finding Paradise

*Then he said, "Jesus, remember me when you come into
your kingdom." And Jesus answered, "I tell you truly,
this day you will be with me in paradise."*
LUKE 23:42–43 PHILLIPS

*D*eath. It's a topic we tend to avoid. And it's a condition our bodies fight. Yet as much as we try not to think about it concerning ourselves and our loved ones, death is a reality in this earthly life.

But as believers, we need not be frightened about the demise of our physical bodies. Because Jesus has, as in all things, already taken care of our destiny.

At the end of His own earthly life, Jesus was hanging on the cross between two thieves. His confused disciples had scattered, wondering what had happened to the kingdom Jesus had talked about. They'd thought it would be a physical realm, not a spiritual one. The women who had hung around the foot of the cross were distraught, weeping, wondering what the future would bring without their beloved leader in it. The soldiers and crowds were mocking Jesus, as was one of the two thieves hanging on their own crosses, one to the left, the other to the right of Jesus.

Yet the second thief, a repentant soul, one who realized the error of his ways, believed in Jesus at the end. In fact, he reprimanded the first criminal for mocking the Lord. For he knew he and his fellow thief were guilty but Jesus was innocent. So he asked Jesus to remember him when He came into His kingdom. And Jesus, while He was suffering the torturous pain of the cross, comforted the man, reassuring him with these words: "I tell you truly, this day you will be with me in paradise" (Luke 23:43).

Paradise. This is the one and only time Jesus uses this word. It relates to the ideal state of bliss realized when we are brought to God's side. It hearkens back to the garden of Eden, before the Fall, when nothing stood between humans and God. It represents deliverance from fear, sorrow, pain, tears, eternal death.

Death is nothing to fear when you trust and believe in the bliss you will encounter as you find yourself at God's side. For the cross has opened a doorway to your final destination—a paradise you can only imagine.

Because I believe in You, Jesus, I have nothing to fear from death.
Help me hang on to this truth every moment of the day. Use it as a balm
to heal the sorrow I feel when I am faced with the death of those
I love. Make my everyday prayer, "Jesus, remember me
when You come into Your kingdom." Amen.

Heart Treasure: In Jesus, I find paradise.

Finding Your Dream

*May God, who puts all things together, makes all things whole, who made
a lasting mark through the sacrifice of Jesus. . .who led Jesus, our Great
Shepherd, up and alive from the dead, now put you together,
provide you with everything you need to please him.*
HEBREWS 13:20–21 MSG

*Y*ou have a dream, something you long to do. Others have encouraged
you to make that dream a reality. But you're uncertain if this is the
path for you. So the question is: Have you asked God?

King David of the Old Testament—a type of Christ and one of Jesus'
ancestors—had a dream, an idea. Once his own house was built, he said
to the prophet Nathan, "I've got this really nice house, but the ark of
God is still under a tent." Thinking David wanted to build a house for God,
Nathan told David, "Whatever is on your heart, go and do it; God is with
you" (1 Chronicles 17:2 MSG).

But that night God told Nathan that David was not the one to build
God a new house. In fact, He didn't need one—nor had He asked for one.
But because David's heart was in the right place, God would make *David's*
house—and make it an eternal one! Through David would be a dynasty, a
kingdom that would last forever. He was talking about Jesus!

In his prayer of thanks to God for this news, David said, "What more
can I say to you about the way you have honored me? You know what your
servant is really like. For the sake of your servant, O LORD, and according
to your will, you have done all these great things and have made them
known" (1 Chronicles 17:18–19 NLT).

The point here is that whatever your dream is, run it by God. Make
sure that what you intend is what God actually wants you to do. For your
dream is not just yours. It's God's as well. He puts all things together.

God knows you. He knows your heart, your ways, your talents, your means. He has a plan for your life (Jeremiah 29:11). And He will "provide you with everything you need to please him" (Hebrews 13:21 MSG), to make your and His dream a reality.

And this isn't a once-and-done asking. Every step of the way, check in with your fellow Dreamer, the One who has the eternal perspective. When you do, you'll be amazed at the ways God honors you.

God, You have a plan for my life. But I'm a bit confused, wondering if my plan and Your plan for me mesh. Speak to me, Lord. Show me the path You would have me take. Provide me with what I need to please You. Jesus, lead me every step of the way, I pray.

Heart Treasure: In Jesus, I find my dream.

Finding the Right Outlet

Then Jesus went to work on his disciples. "Anyone who intends to come
with me has to let me lead. . . . What kind of deal is it to get everything
you want but lose yourself? What could you ever trade your soul for?"
MATTHEW 16:24, 26 MSG

You may have some days when your nerves are frazzled. Not only that, but running from place to place has left you exhausted. Your eyes ache from the glare of your cell phone, tablet, computer, and television screens. When dinnertime comes, you barely have enough energy to lift the fork to your mouth, much less clean up afterward then plan tomorrow's meals and that day's schedule. When it comes time for bed, you fall into it and can barely lift yourself up and out of it when the morning light streams through your window. You begin to wonder how you'll ever meet the challenges and tasks that lie before you and your tired self.

Author Anne Lamott wrote, "Almost everything will work again if you unplug it for a few minutes, including you."

Hmm. When was the last time you "unplugged" from the world and hung out with Jesus? When was the last time you actually let Him lead you through your day?

Jesus tells His followers that they need to look to Him to guide them through this life. He warns them that if they keep chasing after what the world thinks they should have, they'll be trading their souls for a material existence. And it's so not worth it!

What have you been trading your soul for? Material things? Status? Fame? Fortune?

None of those things will save your life, that's for sure.

So consider re-evaluating your day, your schedule, your priorities. Consider thinking about how much you're relying on things other than Jesus. Instead of letting those things truss you up, consider "trusting up" in Jesus. Delving into His Word. Making it a part of your life. Breathing in the wisdom only He can provide. Letting in the light only He can shine.

Unplug from the world and plug into Jesus. He'll rewire your frazzled nerves. He'll be your buffer against any shock that comes your way. He'll engineer the day that lies before you. He'll make things flow like they never have before. Give Him your mind, your heart, your thoughts, your very being. And He'll plug you into God, the true source of never-ending power.

Oh Jesus, I have been so immersed in what the world wants that I've become frazzled. Help me unplug from the world and plug into You. Be my buffer. Engineer the day that lies before me. Make Your light flow from You through me. In this moment I turn my entire being over to You. Fill me with a heavenly never-ending power. In Your name I pray, amen.

Heart Treasure: In Jesus, I find the right outlet.

Finding Insight

*Once more Jesus addressed the crowd. He said, I am the Light
of the world. He who follows Me will not be walking in
the dark, but will have the Light which is Life.*

JOHN 8:12 AMPC

The world can be a mysterious place. Things are hidden here—traps
and treasures. And often we're unsure of our step, unsure which
way to turn.

We wonder and worry about a bleak financial future. *Where will the
next dollar come from? Should I look for a better-paying job? Is there even
one out there? Is this the right time for a move? What about benefits? What
if I find and take a new job and then get laid off? How will I ever provide for
me and mine?*

Thinking about finances can leave us reeling in heart and mind. We
feel as if we're in the darkness, groping for a wall, trying to find our way
out before we fall into a trap and lose it all. Yet then we may start moving
further in, hoping this was the best decision, perhaps thinking the treasure
we seek will appear right around the corner.

But there's another way. It's through, in, and with Jesus. In Him, we
find the light we need. Because He is the Light of the World, we can be
sure that if we're following Him (instead of the world and its ways), we'll
find the insight, the wisdom, to make the right decision. For in His light,
all is revealed: "In Him all the treasures of [divine] wisdom (comprehensive
insight into the ways and purposes of God) and [all the riches of spiritual]
knowledge and enlightenment are stored up and lie hidden" (Colossians
2:3 AMPC).

The more time we spend with Jesus and His Word, the more we glean
insight into what God and His ways are all about! It doesn't get any better
than that.

As believers, we have faith that Jesus, the Light, will lead us out of whatever darkness, financial or otherwise, we're in. We believe He knows the way—to God, to peace, to joy, to eternal life. So that's our head knowledge. Now our feet need to obey, following Him wherever He leads, knowing He will light the way ahead, and in fact goes ahead before us. And so we can keep walking without fear.

What are your concerns today? What darkness can Jesus' light dispel? What insights have you found in God's Word? Take them to heart and head, and allow Jesus to lead you into the light of life.

Lord, thank You for Your light and wisdom and the insight You provide as I walk this earthly path. Dispel whatever darkness the world throws into my life. Keep the path open and clear as I seek Your face and Your knowledge deep in the mystery of Your Word. Amen.

Heart Treasure: In Jesus, I find insight.

Finding What You Seek

"Keep on asking, and you will receive what you ask for. Keep on seeking,
and you will find. Keep on knocking, and the door will be opened to you.
For everyone who asks, receives. Everyone who seeks, finds.
And to everyone who knocks, the door will be opened."
MATTHEW 7:7–8 NLT

*Y*ou've desired a house, a child, an income. But time after time, you are faced with disappointment. You wonder where you may have gone wrong, what you are to do next.

Jesus provides the answer. He says you're not to give up. You're not to ask just once and then walk away. You're to keep on asking, and asking, and asking.

You're also not to seek just once. But to keep on seeking. When you lose your car keys, you don't stop looking after you've checked your pockets or your purse. No, you become doggedly determined to find them. For you know that if you keep on seeking, you *will* find them.

And lastly, you're not to knock just once to have a door opened to you. You are to keep on knocking, knocking, knocking. Your persistence will get you into where you want to be.

If you continue asking, seeking, and knocking, the prayer will be answered, the treasure found, the door opened. For Jesus tells us that Father God wants you to have what is good for you to have. He will not leave you hanging but will move heaven and earth to grant your prayer.

So how is your prayer life? How intense is your desire? How great is your belief that this triple formula of asking, seeking, and knocking (ASK) has the power Jesus claims it has?

Jesus doesn't make promises and not keep them. Neither does God. Joshua 21:45 (ESV) says, "Not one word of all the good promises that the LORD had made to the house of Israel had failed; all came to pass."

Believe in Jesus' words. Claim God's promises. Neither will ever fail you.

Go to God in prayer. Ask and continue asking, seek and continue seeking, knock and continue knocking. For, as E. M. Bounds wrote, "Prayer moves the hand that moves the world."

Continue to be patient, endure, and have faith. "Patient endurance is what you need now, so that you will continue to do God's will. Then you will receive all that he has promised" (Hebrews 10:36 NLT).

God *will* answer your prayer.

Lord, I'm filled with disappointment when I fail to receive what I think You want me to have. Help me not to get discouraged but to keep coming to You in prayer, asking, seeking, and knocking until I receive, find, and have the door opened. Give me patience and joy as I persist in prayer. In Jesus' name. Amen.

Heart Treasure: In Jesus, I find what I seek.

Finding Your Focus

*Keep your eyes on Jesus, who both began and finished this race
we're in. Study how he did it. Because he never lost sight of
where he was headed—that exhilarating finish in and with
God—he could put up with anything along the way.*
HEBREWS 12:2 MSG

Have you ever heard someone say, "So many things are happening in my life, I don't even have time to think"? Perhaps you've even said it yourself. These words tend to trip off your lips when you've become sucked into all that's going on around you, overpowered by what's coming against you. Then, in the midst of an overwhelming frenzy, having lost your footing, you begin reacting instead of responding to circumstances.

Overwhelm means to turn upside down, to overthrow. It comes from the root word *whelm*, meaning to submerge completely. But if we're under the water due to circumstances, how can we ever keep our eyes on Jesus?

King Jehoshaphat had a lot of things coming against him. In fact, he had a few armies heading his way. At first, "Jehoshaphat feared," but then he "set himself [determinedly, as his vital need] to seek the Lord" (2 Chronicles 20:3 AMPC). He called all his people to seek God too, and then he prayed before them, asking God questions and affirming God's power and might, knowing that no one was able to stand against Him. He recalled God's earlier victories and expressed his confidence that God would hear his prayer and save his people. He gave God the specific circumstances of the situation. He named names. And then he said the kind of words God longs to hear: "We have no might to stand against this great company that is coming against us. We do not know what to do, but our eyes are upon You" (2 Chronicles 20:12 AMPC).

The result of Jehoshaphat's response to his circumstances and his prayer? He and his people, while singing God's praises, walked out toward the enemy and found that the armies had turned on each other. All that remained was for the king and his people to pick up the spoils.

Follow not just Jehoshaphat's but Jesus' example. Keep your eyes on God—not on the things coming against you. Know that He is the answer. Praise Him for what He is going to do, how He is going to work. And then get ready to reap the rewards!

Lord, thank You for this message of hope, focus, prayer, and praise. Help me not to react to my circumstances but to respond, knowing that You are with me. Because of that, I can face anything that comes against me—and keep my eyes on You!

Heart Treasure: In Jesus, I find my focus.

Finding Success

But Jesus said to them, It is I; be not afraid! [I Am; stop being frightened!]
Then they were quite willing and glad for Him to come into the boat.
And now the boat went at once to the land they had steered
toward. [And immediately they reached the shore toward
which they had been slowly making their way.]
JOHN 6:20–21 AMPC

You've waited for Jesus, but He seems to have gone off somewhere. So you decide to take the boat out by yourself and head for your destination. Although it's pretty dark, you figure that's okay. After all, you're a seasoned fisherwoman. You know the sea, the shores. And you get in the boat.

Once you're underway, the wind picks up. It begins blowing stronger and stronger. The sea gets very rough. You find yourself straining at the oars as the boat reels from side to side. It's taking in water. A thought creeps into your mind: *Perhaps I didn't think this through.* But you're in the thick of it now. There's no choice but to keep rowing as hard as you can. Now you're not even thinking about your destination. Any beach will do. You just want to get out of this alive!

You've made your way a few miles when, through the storm, you suddenly see Jesus walking on the water toward you! You almost can't believe your eyes. Your stomach drops; your heart fills with fear. And then you hear His words: "It's Me! Don't be afraid! I'm here with you!"

Finally, you welcome Jesus into your boat. You're willing for Him to take the seat next to you, sit at the helm, take your oars if He wants them. And then, before you know it, you've arrived at the shore you'd been steering toward all along.

Sound familiar? It happened. To the disciples. At least they had some help rowing. But oftentimes you find yourself alone in this situation. You didn't wait for Jesus. You thought you'd go ahead with your plan anyway.

Perhaps He's busy. After all, the world has so many issues. He may have been needed elsewhere.

Don't believe it! Jesus is everywhere, waiting for you to call out to Him. To ask His advice—with every stroke of the oar. And then when He reaches you, He tells you, "Stop being frightened!" And the most powerful One sits down right next to you!

Invite Jesus into every decision, every moment, every place you are. When you willingly do that, you'll immediately reach the shore to which you—in your own power—had slowly been making your way.

Oh Lord Jesus, without You, I'm lost and tossed. In You alone do I reach the shore toward which I'm heading. Remind me to talk to You before I embark upon any adventure. I want You to steer my life. I will not be afraid, knowing You're with me wherever I am. Amen.

Heart Treasure: In Jesus, I find success.

Finding the God Who Sees

*So she called the name of the Lord who spoke to her, "You are a God of
seeing," for she said, "Truly here I have seen him who looks after me."*
GENESIS 16:13 ESV

*Y*ou're conflicted, not sure which way to turn, what path to take. You
look all around but don't see a way out of your situation. You fear
any step will be a misstep. Finally, the urge to escape your circumstances
wells up from within. So you run. You climb. You try to break free from
all that's coming against you, ashamed of yourself as you do so. *Where's
my courage, my faith?* you think. And as you think it, you're hoping maybe
God is looking the other way.

No matter what's happening, be assured: Jesus sees you. He saw
Nathanael. And He knew all about him before they met face-to-face.
When Nathanael asked Jesus, "How can you know me?" Jesus responded,
"When you were underneath that fig-tree. . .before Philip called you, I saw
you." And Nathanael came back with, "Master, you are the Son of God,
you are the king of Israel!" (John 1:48–49 PHILLIPS).

Jesus also saw Zacchaeus, the thieving tax collector who climbed a
tree to get a good look at Jesus coming through town. When He got to the
foot of the sycamore, Jesus said, "Zacchaeus, hurry up and come down. I
must be your guest today" (Luke 19:5 PHILLIPS).

Jesus is a lot like Father God, who in Old Testament times saw the slave
Hagar being mistreated by her mistress, Sarah. When she was on the run,
heading away from Sarah and into the wilderness, she stopped at a spring
of water. Even though God said, "Where have you come from and where
are you heading?" He knew the answer. He wanted to hear it in Hagar's own
words. She said she was running from Sarah. God told Hagar to go back and
that she would bear a son who would be the father of many. "So she called
the name of the Lord who spoke to her, 'You are a God of seeing,' for she
said, 'Truly here I have seen him who looks after me' " (Genesis 16:13 ESV).

You need never feel lost, alone, conflicted, or directionless. Nor do you ever need to be on the run. Take a deep breath. Know that you have Jesus, who sees you, knows you. And you have Father God, who's watching out for you, over you, and after you. He is the God of seeing.

Lord Jesus, knowing that You see all I do, hear all I say, can be kind of unnerving. Yet I wouldn't have it any other way, for that means You also see all that's happening and can help me find my way. Thank You for looking after me so well. With You and Father God, I'll never be alone.

Heart Treasure: In Jesus, I find the God who sees.

Finding the Power to Face Anything

When you pass through the waters, I will be with you, and through the rivers, they will not overwhelm you. When you walk through the fire, you will not be burned or scorched, nor will the flame kindle upon you.

ISAIAH 43:2 AMPC

$\mathcal{N}$o matter what you may be suffering, Jesus will be with you, will help you find a way through.

That's what He did for three amazing young champions of the faith in Daniel 3. Although this incident occurred over two thousand years ago, it's a story that never gets old.

Shadrach, Meshach, and Abednego had been evicted from their homeland of Judah and transported to Nebuchadnezzar's Babylon. This king set up a golden statue that all were to worship or else be thrown into a fiery furnace. But these three Jews refused to obey Nebuchadnezzar's edict, telling him: "If we are thrown into the blazing furnace, the God whom we serve is able to save us. He will rescue us from your power. . . . But even if he doesn't, we want to make it clear to you. . .that we will never serve your gods or worship the gold statue you have set up" (Daniel 3:17–18 NLT). In his burning rage, the king had the furnace temperature turned up seven times higher than usual. Then the men, fully clothed, were tied up and thrown into the flames. You'd think they'd be goners. But they weren't.

Nebuchadnezzar, looking into the furnace, expecting to see three men aflame, was amazed: "I see four men loose, walking in the midst of the fire, and they are not hurt! And the form of the fourth is like a son of the gods!" (Daniel 3:25 AMPC). As the men came out of the furnace, not only were they unharmed, but their ropes were gone, their clothes were unsinged, and the smell of smoke didn't cling to them.

The astounding sight prompted King Nebuchadnezzar to say, "Blessed be the God of Shadrach, Meshach, and Abednego, Who has sent His angel and delivered His servants who believed in, trusted in, and relied on Him! And they set aside the king's command and yielded their bodies rather than serve or worship any god except their own God" (Daniel 3:28 AMPC).

When you trust that God is with you, that He'll deliver you in whatever way He deems best, that His way will be good for you and all those around you, there's nothing you cannot face. No matter how high the waves of your circumstances or how hot the flames of your suffering, know that God will handle whatever is coming against you. And not only that, He'll be walking with you every step of the way.

Lord Jesus, help me to yield my entire self to You, to trust that You're walking with me every step of the way. With You by my side, I can face anything! Amen!

Heart Treasure: In Jesus, I find the power to face anything!

Finding What's Really Needed

"Martha, my dear, you are worried and bothered about providing so many things. Only a few things are really needed, perhaps only one."
LUKE 10:41–42 PHILLIPS

Are you a Mary, a Martha. . .or a Myrna?

In Luke 10:38–42 we find that Jesus enjoyed spending time with the sisters Mary and Martha. So when He stopped by, Martha welcomed Him with open arms. But then, with a houseful of guests, she soon found herself distracted, encumbered, and "very worried about her elaborate preparations" (Luke 10:40 PHILLIPS). Meanwhile, her sister Mary had "settled down at the Lord's feet and was listening to what he said" (Luke 10:39 PHILLIPS).

Frazzled, Martha said to Jesus, "Lord, don't you mind that my sister has left me to do everything by myself? Tell her to get up and help me!" (Luke 10:40 PHILLIPS).

Jesus responded, "Martha, my dear, you are worried and bothered about providing so many things. Only a few things are really needed, perhaps only one. Mary has chosen the best part and you must not tear it away from her!" (Luke 10:41–42 PHILLIPS).

It's great to welcome Jesus into your life and do things to serve Him and others. The danger lies in putting those things before just *being* with Him, sitting at His feet, hanging on His every word. For that's what you need the most.

So who's Myrna? Well, she represents the woman who drifts on the edges of service for God. She's the pew potato who comes to church, listens to the sermon, and gives her tithe. But when it comes to serving others—either inside or outside the church—or lending a hand to some ministry, she turns the other way. She doesn't lift a finger, her inaction oftentimes prompting many Marthas to emerge, to pick up the slack.

There is no room for judgment here. No one really knows who does what outside of their churchgoing. So we shouldn't point fingers like Martha. But we do need to take a look within and ask Jesus what He would have *us* do, beyond the time we spend with Him just being, hearing, and heeding.

And that's the point, really. Making sure we first of all choose the best part, the one thing really needed: spending time with Jesus. From there, if we are obedient and keep our Jesus-first-above-all mind-set, we'll be led to what He wants us to do—within and without.

Lord Jesus, help me each day to choose the most needful thing—sitting at Your feet, listening to Your words. As I rise from there, show me what You would have me do to serve You and others. In Your name I pray, amen.

Heart Treasure: In Jesus, I find what's really needed.

Finding the Words to Say

Resolve and settle it in your minds not to meditate and prepare beforehand how you are to make your defense and how you will answer. For I [Myself] will give you a mouth and such utterance and wisdom that all of your foes combined will be unable to stand against or refute.
LUKE 21:14–15 AMPC

*H*ave you ever found yourself tongue-tied when someone asks you about your faith, beliefs, or Jesus? Have you been afraid of saying the wrong thing and so said nothing—or even worse, denied knowing Jesus? And then regretted it?

You're not alone. The disciple Peter tripped over his tongue. Three times. It was after Jesus had been arrested and the soldiers were marching Him off to the house of the high priest. "Peter followed at a distance" (Luke 22:54 PHILLIPS). Next, he sat down with some people who were gathered around a fire in the courtyard. When they started asking questions, Peter at first denied knowing Jesus. Then he denied being one of His followers. Finally, he denied even hanging with Jesus. *While* Peter was giving this third and final false testimony, a rooster crowed. "The Lord turned his head and looked straight at Peter, and into his mind flashed the words that the Lord had said to him. . .'You will disown me three times before the cock crows today.' And he went outside and wept bitterly" (Luke 22:61–62 PHILLIPS).

All this happened *after* Jesus had given the disciples—including Peter—some wisdom for how to handle themselves in such instances, telling them He or the Holy Spirit would give them the right words at just the right time (Luke 12:11–12; 21:14–15).

The good news is that even though Peter denied Jesus three times, Jesus not only forgave him but didn't bring it up in their later conversation on the beach (John 21). It's as if He'd forgotten all about it. Instead of holding those denials against Peter, Jesus asked him three times if he loved Him. When Peter responded with yes three times, Jesus gave him the responsibility of feeding and caring for His sheep!

When you mess up by not fessing up to your love for and devotion to Jesus, don't continue kicking yourself. Jesus sees, hears, knows what's happened. But He still has a plan for you. You're still His hands, feet, and mouth in this earthly realm. And the next time someone gives you the opportunity to claim that you know the Son of God, don't worry about how you'll respond. Just say a quick prayer, tune in to Jesus, and let Him give you the words to say.

Sometimes, Lord, I find myself tongue-tied with fear when people ask me about You. Help me rest in the knowledge that all I need to do is tune in to You, and Your Spirit will give me Your wisdom and the words You want me to say.

Heart Treasure: In Jesus, I find the words to say.

Finding a Wonder-Filled Day

God created everything through him, and nothing was created
except through him. The Word gave life to everything that
was created, and his life brought light to everyone.

JOHN 1:3–4 NLT

*J*t's another day. Just like yesterday. The routines lie before you. Clothes to be cleaned, dried, folded. Dishes to be washed, dried, put away. Meals and beds to be made. Snow to be shoveled, grass cut, a garden weeded. A job to be driven to, performed, then driven home from. Kids to be sent off to school, picked up, fed, washed, and put to bed. Calls to be made. The list goes on and on. And you haven't even gotten out of bed yet.

Author Paulo Coelho wrote, "If you think adventure is dangerous, try routine—it's lethal." Hmm. Sounds as if seeing your life as one big routine can be bad for your health. Sounds as if an attitude adjustment, a new perspective, is imperative when you feel like a hamster running endlessly on the wheel of life.

So how do you get off the wheel? First, if you feel you're stuck in a routine, thank God for it. Because that means no upheaval is in your life right now. And that can be a good thing. So thank God for that routine, for all your current blessings!

Second, consider having Maya Angelou's daybreak attitude: "This is a wonderful day. I've never seen this one before." Realize that every day is different. And it is—and will be even more so if you remember that Jesus is *with* you in all you do. Even better than that, He is *in* everything—including your routine! Look for His light all around you, that light that "shines on in the darkness, for the darkness has never overpowered it [put it out or absorbed it or appropriated it, and is unreceptive to it]" (John 1:5 AMPC). Then spread that wondrous light.

The prophet Isaiah wrote, "How beautiful upon the mountains are the feet of him who brings good news, who publishes peace, who brings good news of happiness, who publishes salvation, who says to Zion, 'Your God reigns' " (Isaiah 52:7 ESV). Those feet, the ones at the bottom of your legs, may not be the most beautiful physically; but they can be spiritually, when you look at your day, your life, your routine as a blessing from God in the light of Jesus—and then pass that good news, that light, that blessing on to others.

Today is a new day, a new beginning. Keep your eyes open for Jesus. Absorb His light. Then radiate that light to all you meet—yourself included.

Thank You, Jesus, for shining Your light into my day, for Your many blessings, for the adventure of living a life with You. Help me spread Your love and light into the world around me. Give me the beautiful feet that bring good news—not just today but every day!

Heart Treasure: In Jesus, I find a wonder-filled day.

Finding Love over Judgment

"Don't pick on people, jump on their failures, criticize their faults—unless, of course, you want the same treatment. That critical spirit has a way of boomeranging."

MATTHEW 7:1–2 MSG

*R*ight after telling people to love each other (even their enemies), have mercy, and forgive, Jesus tells them not to judge each other. To explain this, He uses a great hyperbole—an extreme and intentional exaggeration—to make His point, saying, "How can you say to your brother, 'Brother, let me take out the speck that is in your eye,' when you yourself do not see the log that is in your own eye? You hypocrite, first take the log out of your own eye, and then you will see clearly to take out the speck that is in your brother's eye" (Luke 6:42 ESV).

Eek. Jesus has a way of cutting right to the heart of the matter, doesn't He? Giving us even more pause is His idea that being critical of someone else has a way of coming right back to us (Matthew 7:1).

But it's not just because our words of judgment can boomerang that we shouldn't judge others. It's because when we criticize others with our words, it stops up the love and encouragement we could be extending. Mother Teresa put it this way: "If you judge people, you have no time to love them."

So how do we keep from judging and instead speak words of love and encouragement? Author Suzanne Woods Fisher gives us a hint: "We fail in the work of grace and love when there is too much of us and not enough of God." That sounds familiar, doesn't it? That's because John the Baptist, the forerunner of Jesus, the one crying in the wilderness, said it in his own way in John 3:30 (AMPC): "He must increase, but I must decrease. [He must grow more prominent; I must grow less so]." *The Message* gives us further insight with its paraphrase: "This is the assigned moment for him to move into the center, while I slip off to the sidelines."

When words of judgment and criticism start building up behind your teeth, pause. Slip yourself off to the side. Allow Jesus to move to the center of your heart, mind, spirit, and mouth. Remember how much He loves you, how imperfect you must seem in His eyes. Then watch Him exchange your criticisms with His words and thoughts, His spirit of love, mercy, and forgiveness. That's a boomerang effect you can get behind!

Lord Jesus, thank You for allowing me to be a conduit of Your mercy and forgiveness. Help me to have more of You than me within and without. Transform my words of judgment into Your words of love and encouragement. In Your name I pray, amen.

Heart Treasure: In Jesus, I find love over judgment.

Finding That Prayer and Praise Trump Panic

*As Paul and Silas were praying and singing hymns of praise to God,
and the [other] prisoners were listening to them, suddenly there was
a great earthquake, so that the very foundations of the prison
were shaken; and at once all the doors were opened
and everyone's shackles were unfastened.*
ACTS 16:25–26 AMPC

Author Rachel Wojo says, "Prayer trumps panic. Every. Time." And that's true. But something else trumps panic as well: praise.

When Paul and Silas were in prison, they didn't just pray; they sang hymns of praise to God. What faith! To be locked in jail and bound by chains and yet to actually praise God! Amazing. But that's what it took to shake up not just those who were listening to them, but the very foundation of their prison. That was the formula needed to open their doors and release their shackles.

And their prayers and praise didn't release just *them* but also the jailer, who was literally shaken up, thinking the prisoners had escaped. Once Paul told him not to worry, that all were there and accounted for, the jailer ended up collapsing in front of Paul and Silas, asking what he needed to do to be saved. They replied, "Believe in the Lord Jesus Christ [give yourself up to Him, take yourself out of your own keeping and entrust yourself into His keeping] and you will be saved" (Acts 16:31 AMPC). Then they told him about Jesus. In response, the jailer dressed the wounds of Paul and Silas and made them as comfortable as he could. In the end, not only were the jailer and his household baptized, but every member had put his or her trust in God. And Paul and Silas were soon out of jail—free!

What an eye—and door—opener! This story is not fiction. It's an actual account of what happened about two thousand years ago to two believers who totally relied on their Lord and Savior Jesus Christ. And it can happen to you.

Instead of panicking when you're in a situation from which you feel there's no escape, take it to Jesus. Subdue your racing heart with prayer and praise, knowing He'll work things out. In the process, He will save not just you but everyone else in your situation who's imprisoned in fear and shackled by anxiety.

Prayer and praise will transform your circumstances in ways that exceed your greatest expectations.

Lord Jesus, I come to You in prayer—and praise! For when I do, I know and trust that You'll remedy whatever situation I find myself in. That You'll free me from whatever is holding me down. Give me the courage to vocalize my love for and belief in You, no matter where I am or who is with me. For when I do so, You'll free them as well. In Your name, amen.

Heart Treasure: In Jesus, I find that prayer and praise trump panic every time!

....

....

....

....

....

....

....

....

....

Finding the Safety of God's Will

When they were both aboard the boat, the wind dropped.
The whole crew came and knelt down before Jesus,
crying, "You are indeed the Son of God!"
MATTHEW 14:32–33 PHILLIPS

*I*s there some kind of fear preventing you from taking a risk? Have doubts turned your feet to clay, keeping you from moving forward?

After feeding the five thousand, Jesus insisted His disciples get into their boat and cross the lake while He dismissed the people. Then He went up the mountain to be alone with God and pray. Hours later, the boat was far out to sea, and the disciples were having trouble battling the waves. So Jesus took a walk out there.

Seeing what they thought was a ghost, the disciples were terrified and screamed out in fear. But Jesus immediately said, "It's all right! It's I myself, don't be afraid!" (Matthew 14:27 PHILLIPS). Peter came back with, "Lord, if it's really you. . .tell me to come to you on the water" (verse 28 PHILLIPS). Jesus told him to come, so Peter boldly stepped out of the boat and walked on the water, heading toward Jesus. But when he took his eyes off the Lord and looked at the tumultuous waves, he panicked and started to sink. He cried out for Jesus to save him. "At once Jesus reached out his hand and caught him, saying, 'You little-faith! What made you lose your nerve like that?' " (Matthew 14:31 PHILLIPS).

Someone once said, "The safest place to be is within the will of God." If only Peter had clung to that buoy of faith! If only he'd kept his eyes on Jesus, he'd have found his sea legs and made it over to Jesus' side.

It's rarely easy to take a risk. But when you think you're being called to come out and take a chance, and you know the voice calling you is that of Jesus, remember that wherever you're walking, you're within the will of God. And there's no safer place to be, for God has His eye on you:

"I [the Lord] will instruct you and teach you in the way you should go; I will counsel you with My eye upon you" (Psalm 32:8 AMPC). He won't let you fall: "Stalwart walks in step with GOD; his path blazed by GOD, he's happy. If he stumbles, he's not down for long; GOD has a grip on his hand" (Psalm 37:23–24 MSG).

Lord Jesus, what a relief knowing that if I'm heading toward where You're calling, You'll be there waiting with open arms. You have a grip on my hand. You'll be helping me, leading me, step by step. Help me take to heart the truth that when I'm with You and in Your will, I'm as safe as I can be.

Heart Treasure: In Jesus, I find the safety of God's will.

Finding the Ultimate Steadfast Companion

"Look! I stand at the door and knock. If you hear my voice and open the door, I will come in, and we will share a meal together as friends."
REVELATION 3:20 NLT

*P*eople come and go in our lives. Our high school friends are replaced by college chums, who later are replaced by coworkers. Our siblings eventually grow up, leave home, and move away. We might marry, have children of our own. Then they too may move out, marry, and begin their own families, leaving us as empty nesters.

Whether our houses are empty of friends, parents, children, or spouses or we're bursting at the seams with little ones and big ones, we still may find ourselves experiencing a strange ache of loneliness.

Are you pining for a partner, for the companionship of one who knows and loves you like no other? Rest assured, Jesus has never left you nor forsaken you. He wants to spend time with you. In Revelation 3:20 (NLT), He says, "Look! I stand at the door and knock. If you hear my voice and open the door, I will come in, and we will share a meal together as friends."

When you feel all alone in this world, as if no one understands you, open the door and let Jesus in. When you have lost someone very dear to you and you feel no one will ever replace him or her, open the door and let Jesus in. When the kids have left and your voice seems to echo in the emptiness of their rooms, open the door and let Jesus in.

Ralph Waldo Emerson, philosopher and poet, wrote, "God enters by a private door into each individual." But He won't force His way in. He's waiting for you to reach for that knob and open it. Not just a crack but all the way!

Listen for Jesus. Know that He's right on the other side of that door you may not even realize you'd closed. Open it, knowing that when you do, you'll be letting in the light you need, gaining a friendship like no other. As *Matthew Henry's Commentary* puts it, "Those who open to him shall enjoy his presence. . . . He will sup with them; he will accept of what is good in them. . .and he will bring the best part of the entertainment with him."

Let Jesus into your heart and you'll have found the ultimate companion, the One who will never leave or forsake you.

To imagine that You're on the other side of the door, knocking, just waiting for me to turn the knob and let You in, is amazing, Lord Jesus. I'm opening the door of my heart now, Lord. Come in and spend time with me. Remind me that You're always close. And that it is up to me to let You into every moment of my day and life. Amen.

Heart Treasure: In Jesus, I find the ultimate steadfast companion.

Finding Contentment

I have learned in any and all circumstances the secret of facing every situation. . . . I have strength for all things in Christ Who empowers me [I am ready for anything and equal to anything through Him Who infuses inner strength into me].

PHILIPPIANS 4:12–13 AMPC

A farmer had a stallion that escaped its paddock. The neighbors said to the man, "We're sorry to hear the bad news that your horse ran off." The farmer replied, "Good or bad, hard to say."

The next day the horse returned with seven wild horses. Hearing the news, the neighbors said, "That's good!" The farmer replied, "Good or bad, hard to say."

Days later, the farmer's son was breaking in one of the wild horses and fell off, injuring his leg. After the cast was put on, the neighbors said, "Heard about your son breaking his leg. That's bad." The farmer said, "Good or bad, hard to say."

Weeks later, the king's men came around to recruit soldiers to fight in the war. But the farmer's son wasn't taken because he had a broken leg. The neighbors came to the farmer and said, "That's good." He responded, "Good or bad, hard to say."

You didn't get the job you interviewed for. Good or bad? Hard to say. You *did* get the job you interviewed for. Good or bad? Hard to say. You didn't get the house you put an offer on. Good or bad? Hard to say. You *did* get the house. Good or bad? Hard to say.

The Old Testament patriarch Joseph went through many trials. Good or bad, it's hard to say. But whatever he went through, God was with him. And because Joseph *knew* God was with him, he not only remained content but continued to prosper. And as it turned out, each of Joseph's trials helped him acquire skills that enabled him to become a leader *and* save his family.

Don't let disappointment or discouragement impede your progress. Instead, see things as neither good nor bad. Like the apostle Paul, author of Philippians, learn to be content whatever your circumstances. Because no matter what you're facing, God is with you and Christ is empowering you. No matter what your circumstances, God is preparing you so that you'll be able to handle bigger challenges down the road.

Whatever happens—good or bad, hard to say—just be content in God, pray, and let Christ have His way.

Lord Jesus, help me not to whine or complain about my circumstances, not to be hung up on whether things look good or bad. Remind me to simply pray and let You have Your way. And I will find that contentment I crave as Your strength permeates my very being, helping me to become the woman You created me to be.

Heart Treasure: In Jesus, I find contentment.

Finding a Resulting Peace

"This is your Father you are dealing with, and he knows better than you what you need. With a God like this loving you, you can pray very simply. Like this: Our Father in heaven. . . set the world right; do what's best—as above, so below."
MATTHEW 6:8–10 MSG

*Y*ou've developed a perfect plan. You've taken all the right steps, set everything in place. Now all you have to do is watch your vision come to fruition. You've determined that your plan cannot fail and you'll gain exactly what you've aimed to obtain!

Hmm. Sounds like something may be missing in this game plan.

King David's warrior Joab had a plan when kingdoms came to battle the Israelites. "Joab. . .chose some of the best men of Israel and arrayed them against the Syrians. The rest of his men he put in the charge of Abishai his brother, and they were arrayed against the Ammonites" (1 Chronicles 19:10–11 ESV). Joab had taken all the right steps, set everything in place. He even had a backup plan, telling his brother, "If the Syrians are too strong for me, then you shall help me, but if the Ammonites are too strong for you, then I will help you" (1 Chronicles 19:12 ESV). Then he added, "Be strong, and let us use our strength. . .and may the LORD do what seems good to him" (1 Chronicles 19:13 ESV). There's the clincher! There's what's missing from your plan—leaving the outcome up to God, desiring Him to do what He thinks best!

That's what the Lord's Prayer tells us to do. We're to say to God, "*Your* will be done—not mine." For when we leave our plans up to God, their outcomes are the eternally right ones.

Jesus knew that. That's why He prayed in the garden, "I want your will to be done, not mine" (Luke 22:42 NLT). After those words left His mouth, "an angel from heaven appeared and strengthened him" (Luke 22:43 NLT).

When you plan, you are wise to consider all the steps and implement them as well as to do your best to cover all contingencies. But don't leave out the most important part of every plan: asking the Lord to do His will, to "do what seems good to him." For then you will have His peace no matter what the results.

Help me remember, Lord, to put all my plans and their outcomes into Your good hands. For when I do, I receive not only Your peace but Your strength and joy. So I pray right here and now, in all areas of my life, that You take all I am and all I have and do whatever seems good to You. In Jesus' name, amen.

Heart Treasure: In Jesus, I find a resulting peace.

Finding God Revealed

"This is your Father you are dealing with, and he knows better than you what you need. With a God like this loving you, you can pray very simply. Like this: Our Father in heaven, reveal who you are."
MATTHEW 6:8–9 MSG

With a heavy heart, you get ready for bed. You lie down but find sleep elusive. Your troubles have your mind racing, turning over possible outcomes and avenues of relief.

Not sure where to turn? Look to God. Allow Him to reveal Himself to you.

Go before Him. "Just be there as simply and honestly as you can manage. The focus will shift from you to God, and you will begin to sense his grace" (Matthew 6:6 MSG).

The author of Psalm 77 was lying sleepless in bed when his thoughts turned toward God: "When I remember God, I moan; when I meditate, my spirit faints" (Psalm 77:3 ESV).

All the promises God had made to His people—to him—began to seep into the psalmist's mind. He recalled how things in his life were once better, easier: "I consider the days of old, the years long ago. I said, 'Let me remember my song in the night; let me meditate in my heart' " (Psalm 77:5–6 ESV). And then he searched for what was really in his heart, the questions he really wanted God to answer, saying, "Then my spirit made a diligent search" (Psalm 77:6 ESV).

Finally, he strengthened himself, giving himself peace by thinking back to all the things God had done for His people: "I will remember the deeds of the LORD; yes, I will remember your wonders of old. I will ponder all your work, and meditate on your mighty deeds" (Psalm 77:11–12 ESV).

When you're so down you don't know what to do, when your nights are sleepless, when your days are spent wandering around in a fog of confusion, when you're disturbed within, seeing no way out, ask God to reveal Himself to you. Ask Him the hard questions. Then remember what He has done for you in the past—and how He performed many amazing deeds to rescue all His people. Meditate on His promises, His good Word. Allow your focus to shift from your troubles to the ultimate promise—Jesus, the revelation of God. Then feel His grace rain down upon you.

Remember. Meditate. Then celebrate the God who reveals Himself to you today. And will do so tomorrow.

When I'm lost in a sea of troubles, be my lifeboat, Jesus. Help me to remember all the times You've rescued me. Help me to meditate on all the amazing promises found in God's Word. Guide me to all wisdom and comfort as I shift my focus to You. And raise me up as I sense Your grace.

Heart Treasure: In Jesus, I find God revealed.

Finding Victory

"I am the Lord, and there is no other, besides me there is no God; I equip you. . .that people may know, from the rising of the sun and from the west, that there is none besides me; I am the Lord, and there is no other. I form light and create darkness. . .I am the Lord, who does all these things."
ISAIAH 45:5–7 ESV

Sometimes we find ourselves facing a Goliath of a problem. The giant stands before us, taunting us, daring us to take one step forward, calling us weaklings. Before we know it, we start to think we cannot stand up against it.

David had the same issue when he faced Goliath, the giant Philistine no soldier wanted to stand up to. And here was David, a mere shepherd boy. What chance did he have against this mighty foe?

But that didn't stop the physically scrawny David. He remembered what God had done for him in the past, how He'd enabled David to kill predators intending to harm his sheep. He pushed aside the brothers who tried to discourage him. When King Saul questioned David's fighting experience, the boy told him, "God, who delivered me from the teeth of the lion and the claws of the bear, will deliver me from this Philistine" (1 Samuel 17:37 MSG). When Saul tried to fit him in more suitable battle gear, David pushed it aside, more comfortable in his own attire. Then he picked up five smooth stones and his sling. He walked out onto the battlefield and, while still hearing Goliath's taunts, put a stone in his sling, sending it through the air and bringing the Goliath problem down with a thump.

No matter how giant the problem you're facing, God is bigger. With Him on your side, you cannot help but have victory.

Consider the apostle Paul, who, after speaking out for Jesus, was threatened with violence. For his own safety, a soldier forcibly committed him to the barracks. "The following night the Lord stood by him and said, 'Take courage' " (Acts 23:11 ESV), words that gave Paul the encouragement he needed, equipping him to face and have victory over whatever was to come.

Know that in the midst of your challenge, Jesus is standing by you. He's there to give you all the courage and encouragement you need to face it. Remember all the ways God has equipped you in the past, brought you out of the fire and the storm, the darkness and the raging waves. There's nothing you cannot do, no victory you cannot gain, with God.

With You by my side, Lord Jesus, I have all the courage, strength, and power I need. Equip me now to face the problems and challenges lying before me. In Your name I pray, amen.

Heart Treasure: In Jesus, I find victory.

Finding Your Thoughts Illuminated

The thief comes only in order to steal and kill and destroy.
I came that they may have and enjoy life, and have
it in abundance (to the full, till it overflows).
JOHN 10:10 AMPC

*D*on't you hate it when negative thoughts creep into your mind and take over? Next thing you know, that narrative running through your head not only is affecting everything you put your hand to but is keeping you from doing what God has called you to do! But take heart! You're not alone.

Consider Moses. He told God he couldn't speak for his people because of his speech impediment (Exodus 4:10–11). Then there was Gideon, who claimed he couldn't save God's people because he was the least of his clan (Judges 6:15). Even Elijah became so depressed, felt so insignificant and tired, that he couldn't go on, so he asked God to just let him die (1 Kings 19:4). Jonah went even further. He was so discouraged and upset, he asked God to kill him (Jonah 4:3).

All these people—Moses, Gideon, Elijah, Jonah—were ones God was challenging to move out of their comfort zones. But here's the thing. Before we step out anywhere, before we even take our next breath, we need to be really *hearing*—and then *changing*—the stories we tell ourselves. You know, the ones that have the dark words *not good enough* in them. And the ones that begin with *But Lord* and end with *I can't*.

But why, you moan, *should I work so hard to be aware of and then replace my negative thoughts? I don't think I can do it. Just thinking about it is making me tired already!* Because Jesus wants you to live an abundant life with Him. And you can't live in His sunshine if your thoughts are pushing you back into the shade.

Jesus Christ, your Shepherd, gave *His* life so that you could have a life—an abundant life, overflowing with His blessings, His strength, His power. And He wants you to know that the enemy would like to poison your mind-set—would, in fact, like to destroy your precious life.

So make Jesus and His words, His precepts, His commandments the focus of your thoughts. When you do, you'll have the power, with His help, to take down every stronghold, to "lead every thought and purpose away captive into the obedience of Christ (the Messiah, the Anointed One)" (2 Corinthians 10:5 AMPC). And you'll be positively able to do all God is calling you to do.

I want You and Your light, Lord, to be shining into the recesses of my mind. Help me to take down every negative thought and change it up so that it is obedient to You. May my thoughts be enlightened by Your Word and Your power. In Jesus' name I pray, amen.

Heart Treasure: In Jesus, I find my thoughts illuminated.

Finding Guidance, Strength, and Power

He [thoroughly] opened up their minds to understand the Scriptures.
LUKE 24:45 AMPC

*T*wo heavyhearted followers of Jesus were on the road to Emmaus. Walking along, they discussed how Jesus, whom they'd hoped would rescue them, had been killed. How the women had gone to His tomb that very morning and not found His body. How some angels had told them He was alive!

The next thing they knew, a man began walking with them, asking them what they'd been discussing. That man was Jesus—but God prevented them from recognizing Him. So they told their story, surprised He hadn't yet heard. Afterward, Jesus asked them why they found it so hard to believe all that the prophets had written in the scriptures, reminding them how the writings clearly indicated all that would have to happen before the Messiah would be glorified. He then took them through His Bible, the Old Testament writings, explaining all the things that pointed to Him.

When the threesome reached Emmaus, the two disciples broke bread with Jesus. As He sat down to eat and said the blessing, their eyes were suddenly opened. They recognized their Lord and Savior, Jesus the Christ! Then He disappeared from their midst.

Within the hour, the twosome left Emmaus and returned to the disciples in Jerusalem. Just as they were telling the others their story, Jesus appeared among them, saying, "Peace be with you" (Luke 24:36 MSG). Later He said, " 'All the things written about me in the Law of Moses, in the Prophets, and in the Psalms have to be fulfilled.' He went on to open their understanding of the Word of God, showing them how to read their Bibles this way" (Luke 24:44–45 MSG).

Jesus made clear the importance of reading God's written Word. After all, He *is* the Word! Both the Old and New Testaments point to Him, include Him, predict Him. He's the thread that ties the entire Bible together.

So when you feel lost, pray to Jesus to open your mind, eyes, and heart as you read the Word. Ask the Holy Spirit to remove the veil over the wisdom contained within its pages. Ask God to point out to you the words you need to hear, to take deep within. What treasures you'll reap, what guidance you'll find, what strength and power you'll glean! Take God's words to heart, making them a theme for your life, for a year, for a moment. Find a motto you can cling to throughout your day.

In God's Word, "seek guidance from the LORD" (1 Chronicles 10:14 ESV). After digesting the words of scripture, "stand upright on your feet" (Acts 14:10 ESV).

Open me up, Lord, to the words You want me to hear,
see, and take into my life. Give me the guidance I seek.
Help me use it to stand upright on my feet in Your power.

Heart Treasure: In Jesus, I find guidance, strength, and power.

....

....

....

....

....

....

....

....

....

Finding Your Way to Prayer

Pray all the time; thank God no matter what happens.
This is the way God wants you who belong to Christ Jesus to live.
1 Thessalonians 5:17–18 MSG

*P*rayer—what is it good for? Absolutely *everything!*

In Luke 18:1, Jesus tells us to pray and never give up. In Colossians 4:2 (NLT), Paul writes, "Devote yourselves to prayer with an alert mind and a thankful heart." First Thessalonians 5:17 (ESV) goes even further, telling us to "pray without ceasing." That's a tall order, especially when we're sad, disappointed, depressed, anxious, desperate. Yet praying is exactly what takes us out of ourselves and our darkness and brings us into Christ's light!

But when, how, where, about what, and to whom are we to pray?

When to pray? All the time! When you're driving or riding to work. When you're waking or about to go to bed. When you're watching your brood of kids or nursing a sick child. When you're at the beginning of an adventure or at the end of your rope. When you've suffered a loss or gained a blessing. When you don't know what to do or say.

How to pray? You can kneel, sit, prostrate yourself. You can pray with your hands folded, head bowed. Or you can extend your arms and look up to heaven.

Where to pray? Anywhere! Jonah prayed from the belly of a giant fish. Hard to get much deeper than that. You can pray from a mountaintop or while you're in your secret closet. You can pray from a prison cell or a boardroom. You can pray on the street or in a park. God, who is everywhere, is waiting to hear from you anywhere!

What to pray? Whatever's on your mind. Whatever questions you want answered. Whatever your heart is pleading for. Sometimes it's hard to get the words out. That's okay. The Holy Spirit will translate your groans to God (Romans 8:26). Or just pray God's words right back to Him.

Who to pray to? If you're anxious, ill, or in need, pray to the Lord of Peace (Isaiah 9:6; John 14:27), the Lord of Healing (Exodus 15:22–26; Matthew 8:16–17), or the Lord Will Provide (Genesis 22:8, 13–14; Acts 14:17), respectively. Need guidance or strength? Pray to the Lord Our Shepherd (Psalm 23; Matthew 18:12–13) or the God of Power and Might (Exodus 15:1–2, 11; Isaiah 43:10–13). The list goes on and on. For God has many different aspects, powers, to deliver whatever you need.

The point is to pray along the way, any time of night or day!

I'm awed by how many avenues You provide to prayer, Jesus.
Help me make it more a part of my life, all day, every day,
so that I can grow even closer to You. In Your name I pray, amen.

Heart Treasure: In Jesus, I find my way to prayer.

Finding the Pattern for Life

Walk in the same way in which he walked.
1 JOHN 2:6 ESV

We like following patterns. We can relax into them, knowing that if we follow the instructions, everything will be all right. The dress will fit just right, the afghan will be the right length, the quilt will have just the right colors and shapes, the sweater will be just the right size.

It's the same with recipes. If we get the freshest vegetables, fruits, and meats, and all the ingredients the recipe calls for, dinner should be perfect, everyone will enjoy it, and we'll have nourished our family.

The pattern concept continues when we seek to emulate our parents or our older siblings. We figure that if we follow in their footsteps, we'll find a good life. So we go to school, then perhaps a trade school or college. We get our first job, eventually start our own family. We go on our merry way, thinking we're on the road to success.

But as it turns out, as much as we like following those patterns, recipes, and people, we quickly discover that life can be messy. After cutting and sewing, for some reason the sleeve doesn't turn out right. *Hmm. Must be a faulty pattern.* Or as we're knitting or crocheting, we realize we've run out of yarn. *Hmm. Now what?* Or the recipe we tried was disappointing, not at all what we thought it would be. And the family we aimed to please is just pushing the mush around with their forks. *Hmm. Was I or the recipe at fault?* Or the idea to pattern our life after someone else's has turned into a nightmare. *Wow. I didn't see this coming!*

When our patterns, recipes, and visions of the ideal life go haywire, we may lose our footing. Our once sure steps begin to slip, leaving us uncertain about our next action or path.

Fortunately, we can rest in the knowledge that Jesus has left us with a pattern of how to live. The disciple John wrote, "Those who obey God's word truly show how completely they love him. That is how we know we are living in him. Those who say they live in God should live their lives as Jesus did" (1 John 2:5–6 NLT).

When we begin living as Jesus did—loving God with all His Being and loving others as He did Himself—we have found the perfect pattern, the perfect recipe, the perfect Person, the perfect path for our lives. And we find all things coming out right.

Lord Jesus, I want to follow You as the pattern for my life. For when I do, I know I'm living just as You would have me live. In Your name I pray, amen.

Heart Treasure: In Jesus, I find the pattern for life.

Finding the Power to Level Mountains

> *"This is what the Lord says to Zerubbabel: It is not by force nor by strength, but by my Spirit, says the Lord of Heaven's Armies. Nothing, not even a mighty mountain, will stand in Zerubbabel's way; it will become a level plain before him!"*
>
> ZECHARIAH 4:6–7 NLT

*Y*ou have a mountain in front of you. Just the sheer size is intimidating. Its shadow looms over you. You have no idea how to get around it, go over it, or tunnel through it to the other side. Nor do you see a way to move it.

That mountain may appear in the form of a person. The teenager who won't come home by curfew. The four-year-old who refuses to eat her peas. The husband who doesn't seem to notice you anymore. The mother-in-law who doesn't think you do anything right. The boss who doesn't think you can handle the project.

Or that mountain may appear in the form of some inner obstacle. Your lack of confidence is blocking your way. You don't think you have the strength to tackle a challenge. You don't think you have the talent, the smarts, the determination to take on a new opportunity.

Whatever shape the mountain takes—inner or outer—you think it's an impossible feat to break through it. And, by yourself, it is impossible. But with faith and God, you can and will find a way!

Jesus says so. He said it twice in Matthew (see 17:20; 21:21). It's an echo of an earlier passage from Zechariah. Zechariah was a prophet and a priest. When Zerubbabel, the governor of Judah, was faced with having to rebuild God's temple in Jerusalem over 2,500 years ago, an angel of God gave Zechariah some encouraging words to strengthen Zerubbabel's confidence. The angel said it wasn't Zerubbabel's force or strength that would be able to accomplish such a feat. Rather, God's Spirit would wipe out whatever stood in his way!

Matthew Henry's Commentary says, "When God has work to do, the mountains. . .dwindle into molehills. . . . Faith will remove mountains and make them plains. Christ is our Zerubbabel. . .nothing is too hard for his grace to do."

So the next time you're faced with any kind of mountain, tap into your faith. Call on God, His Spirit, your Brother Jesus. Say, "So, big mountain, who do you think you are? Next to Jesus, you're nothing but a molehill!" So much for *that* mountain!

Thank You, Jesus, for leveling my mountains. Build up my faith so that when I'm faced with any kind of challenge or obstruction, I'll find that nothing can stand in our way! In You I pray, amen.

Heart Treasure: In Jesus, I find the power to level mountains.

Finding Your Prayer Closet

"But when you pray, go away by yourself, shut the door behind you,
and pray to your Father in private. Then your Father,
who sees everything, will reward you."

MATTHEW 6:6 NLT

The noises in this world can be deafening. First there are the things we can turn on: the radio, television, computers, phones, CD and DVD players, etc. Then there are the noises we can't turn off: traffic, sirens, people, barking dogs. Then there are the inner noises, the to-do lists, what-if scenarios, worries, frustrations that fill our thoughts.

But there's relief. Jesus leads us to a place we can go to turn off the noise and tune in to God so that we can hear Him speak to us. It's what some call a prayer closet.

Perhaps you'd like to create your own space for prayer privacy. It may contain a comfy chair with a table that holds a Bible and a notebook with a nice pen. If, when you get there, away from the outer noise, your inner voice kicks in and begins chattering away, you may find it useful to take up something to keep your hands busy—an easy knitting project, for example, or some darning or sewing on of buttons. There are also some pretty neat coloring books you can get to tone down your inner monologue and begin laying a fertile ground for God's words to take root.

If you're a mom, you may be hard-pressed to find time alone. Take heart. It is possible. Susanna Wesley, mother of John and Charles Wesley and eight others, used to tell her kids that if they saw an apron over her head, that meant she was in her prayer closet and not to be disturbed!

Perhaps you don't have the resources for a prayer closet. That's okay. A walk in the park or on the beach can give you the space to get into God's pace. Or perhaps just the drive or train ride to work will prove to be your best closet. Whatever and wherever it is, turn off the noises you have control over—the radio, cell phone, television, etc.—and allow your inner voice to cool down. Then open your mind, heart, spirit, and soul to what God has to say.

No matter what place you pick, start your prayer session with a Bible passage or a devotion, one that speaks to your heart. When you begin with God's Word, He'll lead your thoughts where He wants them to go. And whatever He tells you in the privacy of the space you share will be your wonder-filled reward!

Lord Jesus, help me make it a point to spend quiet time alone with You and God. For when I am there, hearing Your voice is my reward. Amen.

Heart Treasure: In Jesus, I find my prayer closet.

....

....

....

....

....

....

....

....

....

....

....

....

Finding the Confidence of Faith

If you had faith (trust and confidence in God) even [so small] like a grain of mustard seed, you could say to this mulberry tree, Be pulled up by the roots, and be planted in the sea, and it would obey you.
LUKE 17:6 AMPC

*W*orry is easy. We can find a million things to fret over, not the least of which is wondering if we have enough faith! But Jesus can put our minds at rest on this one. He says, "You don't need *more* faith. There is no 'more' or 'less' in faith. If you have a bare kernel of faith, say the size of a poppy seed, you could say to this sycamore tree, 'Go jump in the lake,' and it would do it" (Luke 17:6 MSG).

So it seems it's not the measure of your faith in this instance; it's the sincerity, the genuineness of it. In other words, do you really trust God? Do you believe that what He says goes? Do you have the confidence He'll do what He says He'll do? If so, have you surrendered to His will, and do you pray in accordance with it? And have you entrusted all you are and have to God's keeping? If you can answer yes to all of those questions, then you have enough faith to figuratively tell a tree to come up out of the ground (roots and all) and replant itself in the seabed amid rolling waves and treacherous currents!

If you need to shore up your trust in God, a dip into His Word will do you good. In fact, memorizing a verse or two is always profitable. Here are a few that might help:

- "The Lord of hosts has sworn, saying, Surely, as I have thought and planned, so shall it come to pass, and as I have purposed, so shall it stand" (Isaiah 14:24 AMPC).
- "Only I can tell you the future before it even happens. Everything I plan will come to pass, for I do whatever I wish" (Isaiah 46:10 NLT).

Those are some strong words. And they only sound right coming out of God's mouth.

But remember, that faith you have is a gift from God. "For by grace you have been saved through faith. And this is not your own doing; it is the gift of God, not a result of works, so that no one may boast" (Ephesians 2:8–9 ESV). So embrace that gift. Get in line with God and His will. Have confidence He's in control. Then allow the faith you have to flow through you so that God can do His work in and around you.

Thank You, Lord Jesus, for the gift of salvation and my faith in You. Help me to remember and stand strong in the confidence of God and His plans, to trust in His promises and pray in His will. Amen.

Heart Treasure: In Jesus, I find the confidence of faith.

Finding the Narrow Gate

"Don't look for shortcuts to God. The market is flooded with surefire,
easygoing formulas for a successful life that can be practiced in your
spare time. Don't fall for that stuff, even though crowds of people do.
The way to life—to God!—is vigorous and requires total attention."
MATTHEW 7:13–14 MSG

*Y*ou're running here and there, trying to hold on to everything you have, want, and think you need. But encumbered with so much stuff from this life, chances are you'll have trouble getting through that narrow gate Jesus talks about.

Jesus doesn't want just part of you. He wants all of you. That may mean giving up a few things, letting them fall by the wayside. Or perhaps it's time to do some delegating to friends, coworkers, fellow Christians, or family members.

Perhaps your ego is getting in the way. You're thinking if you don't do it, it won't be done right. So (sigh) you might as well just do it yourself—along with the million other things you've got on your plate.

Now you've reached the point where you're getting downright cranky with those around you. You're dissatisfied with your life, disgruntled, discouraged, dismayed.

What would happen if you just started over? How about writing a list of all the things you do on a daily basis? Next, list all the things you do on a weekly basis, followed by monthly, and yearly. Then pray. Ask God to help you highlight the things that are the most important in *His* eyes. Now see what your list looks like. Whatever is left will slim you down enough to get through that gate. All the rest you can leave in God's hands to divvy up as He wills.

That ministry that's no longer igniting passion in you? Maybe it's time for God to put it in someone else's hands. How about the ministry that's no longer really serving anyone? Maybe it's time to talk to your pastor about that one.

Now, with your new list in hand, you can give God your total attention! No more distractions! Ah, doesn't that feel better already?

And don't worry about all your new free time. Just keep walking down the road Jesus has paved before you. He may want you to just *be* for a while. Later He may point out a need that only you can fill, one you may not even have seen before with those busy-blinders on. But no worries on your part. Where there's His will, He'll find your way.

When I'm feeling overloaded and overwhelmed, Lord, I know You'll be there to help me become less encumbered so I can get through that narrow gate. Give me the wisdom to do what You choose and thus be freed from any distractions that keep me from being with You. In Your name I pray, amen.

Heart Treasure: In Jesus, I find the narrow gate.

Finding the Way of Making Peace

"God blesses those who work for peace,
for they will be called the children of God."
MATTHEW 5:9 NLT

It's not fun to give your husband the silent treatment. It's unpleasant to hold a grudge against a friend. Even worse to feel the sting that injured both ways after a fight with your child. And it can get down-right uncomfortable after a disagreement with your boss. Let's not even talk about relatives who always manage to find just the wrong way to rub you.

So, okay, your husband didn't notice your new haircut, forgot to take out the trash, or has wronged you in some other way. Perhaps your friend shared a secret that was meant for her ears only. Maybe your child did something that made you lose your temper—again. Perhaps your boss made some sort of sexist remark. Or your mother-in-law managed to get into your house and reorganized your spices.

Whatever the infraction, Jesus calls you to be a peacemaker. Although the word *peacemaker* has a nice ring to it, you may feel like cringing when it's time to put peacemaking into action. It may mean admitting you had some part to play in an argument. It may mean something as simple as saying, "Let's talk." It may mean not talking at all, just simply forgiving and forgetting. Or it may even mean saying you're sorry.

Yet if you're to follow the example of the One who made peace between you and God, you too need to put yourself out there. And if you think about it, it's probably more painful *not* to make peace! Because when you're giving the silent treatment, refusing to hear another side of the story, or just plain on the outs with someone else, it becomes difficult to keep your focus on anything other than the rift that's come between you and another child of God.

So consider the rifts that have occurred in your life. Pray that God would give you the compassion to reach out, the courage to broach the breach, the humility to admit you might've been wrong, the creativity to come up with a compromise if necessary. As God has made you whole with the sacrifice and love of Christ, ask Him to make all your relationships whole.

The place to start making peace is within. Release any grudges you may have been holding. Accept God's forgiveness for any sins or mistakes you've been holding on to. And while you're at it, check your heart for any bitterness or resentment you may feel toward God. When you have made peace with yourself and the Lord, then, and only then, reach out to mend the fences beyond yourself. For then people will see that you really are a child of God.

Bring to mind and heart, Lord Jesus, the peacemaking I need to do between You and me. From there help me to make peace with myself. Then give me the courage to heal the rifts between myself and others, beginning with _____.

Heart Treasure: In Jesus, I find the way of making peace.

Finding Full and Complete Rest

For all who have entered into God's rest have rested from their labors, just as God did after creating the world.
So let us do our best to enter that rest.
HEBREWS 4:10–11 NLT

*F*atigue. It can come upon you gradually or hit you like a speeding train. Such exhaustion can affect you physically, emotionally, mentally, and spiritually, leading to sickness, despair, depression, and un-Christlike behavior.

The remedy? Falling into Christ's arms. Allowing Him to carry you. Letting His presence nourish you with His bread and living water.

Jesus, who promised to share your load, asks you to come away with Him, just as He asked the disciples (Mark 6:31). Yet you may say, "I don't have time to rest. Too many things to do, too much on my plate. Maybe tomorrow." But let's make things perfectly clear: even God rested! Okay, granted, it was after He created the world. But remember that you too, a woman made in His likeness, are a creator. Not that you can make anything truly original—God always provides the materials. But even as a re-creator, you need to rest. God says so, even commands that you do so (Exodus 20:8–10). And He's there to help: "Even to your old age I am He, and even to hair white with age will I carry you. I have made, and I will bear; yes, I will carry and will save you" (Isaiah 46:4 AMPC).

Even if you're relatively young, fatigue can still come knocking. "Even youths will become weak and tired, and young men will fall in exhaustion" (Isaiah 40:30 NLT).

But rest assured, God "gives power to the weak and strength to the powerless. . . . Those who trust in the LORD will find new strength. They will soar high on wings like eagles. They will run and not grow weary. They will walk and not faint" (Isaiah 40:29, 31 NLT).

Ah, flying like an eagle, above all the cares of this world. Being renewed by the Lord. That's just what you need. So take a moment now to commune with God. Breathe in His peace and comfort. Then, as soon as you are able, get yourself the rest you need—in God. Turn off the television, put your cell phone on airplane mode, close the book, shut the door, and get into bed. Allow the sleep you need in God to heal you, strengthen you, and renew you.

Lord Jesus, I need to rest in You, to allow the cares of this world to fade away and to get myself a good night's sleep. As I am slumbering, I know You will not only watch over me but renew me—mind, spirit, body, and soul. Thank You for creating, carrying, and caring for me. In Jesus' name I pray, amen.

Heart Treasure: In Jesus, I find full and complete rest.

....

....

....

....

....

....

....

....

....

....

....

Finding the Peace of the Lily

Why are you anxious and troubled with cares. . . ? Consider the lilies,
how they grow. They neither [wearily] toil nor spin nor weave;
yet I tell you, even Solomon in all his glory (his splendor
and magnificence) was not arrayed like one of these.
LUKE 12:26–27 AMPC

Wouldn't it be great to be a lily? They don't work or make their clothing; they don't worry about food and drink; yet they're more beautiful than any outfit Solomon ever wore!

If you were a lily, you wouldn't care where your next meal was coming from nor when you'd find time to make it. Nor would you care about what you were going to drink or when you'd be able to drink it. You wouldn't have to spend time standing at your closet, wondering what you should wear that day. You wouldn't have to earn money, pay the rent, or be concerned about health-care coverage or taxes.

But Jesus says you have an advantage over the lilies—if only you'd stop being weighed down with all kinds of anxieties. If only you'd realize God knows what you need and when you need it.

So how do you get to the point where you no longer worry? Well, first you need to believe what Jesus says. After all, He is the Son of God.

Next you need to trust God totally. Why? Because when you trust God, He gives you perfect peace. The Bible says so: "You will guard him and keep him in perfect and constant peace whose mind [both its inclination and its character] is stayed on You, because he commits himself to You, leans on You, and hopes confidently in You" (Isaiah 26:3 AMPC). Lean into this verse. Study it. To really get it down, here's a simpler version to memorize: "You keep him in perfect peace whose mind is stayed on you, because he trusts in you" (ESV).

And how do you build up that trust? You "delight in the law of the

Lord, meditating on it day and night" (Psalm 1:2 NLT). Why? Because people who do that "are like trees planted along the riverbank, bearing fruit each season. Their leaves never wither, and they prosper in all they do" (Psalm 1:3 NLT).

So, to sum up, believe what Jesus says. Trust God. And build up that trust by spreading your roots deep into God's Word. Then you'll have His perfect peace in this life and the next.

I want to be as anxiety-free as the lily, Jesus, trusting God knows about and will provide everything I need—and beyond. So I'm digging deep into Your Word, Lord, allowing it to nourish my heart, mind, spirit, and soul, and already feel the perfect peace You have promised. Amen.

Heart Treasure: In Jesus, I find the peace of the lily.

Finding the Balm of the Psalms

*He who dwells in the secret place of the Most High shall remain stable
and fixed under the shadow of the Almighty [Whose power no foe can
withstand]. I will say of the Lord, He is my Refuge and my Fortress,
my God; on Him I lean and rely, and in Him I [confidently] trust!*
PSALM 91:1–2 AMPC

Ever have one of those periods in life when you feel like you can't catch your breath? Your mom dies. A month later, your dog dies. Soon after that, your adult son loses his job and ends up moving in with you until he can get back on his feet. About a month later, your pastor decides to resign. By this point, you're so tired, you say to yourself, *Sure, why not?*

What do you do when you keep getting hit by life events that leave you gasping for breath? You fall into the book of Psalms. That's what Jesus did when He was on the cross. He prayed out, "My God, my God, why have you forsaken me?" (Psalm 22:1 ESV).

When you need help, when you want to tell God how you're feeling but can't find the words to express it, the Psalms are just where you need to be. Because not only do you find others who were once just where you are now—or in an even worse place—but you find the hope, strength, and remedy you need.

For example, when you're feeling directionless, anxious, defenseless, you'll find words of comfort in Psalm 23.

If you need strength, turn to Psalm 91. There you'll find how wonderful it is to live "in the secret place of the Most High" where you'll "remain stable and fixed under the shadow of the Almighty [Whose power no foe can withstand]" (verse 1 AMPC). When you're in that place, you need not be afraid. Nothing and no one can harm you, for God will send His angels to protect you. They'll bear you up on their wings.

Psalm 91 goes on to affirm God's love for you, reminding you that He knows your name and exactly what you're going through. That when you call on Him, He'll answer.

So when the going gets tough, go to the book of Psalms, heartfelt words inspired by God and written just for you. Ask the Holy Spirit to guide you to the passages you need to read and heed. And bring Jesus along to illuminate and reinforce the words that heal your heart and strengthen your spirit.

Thank You, Lord, for the gift I find in the words of the psalmists.
Lead me to those I need to heal my heart and strengthen my spirit.
Help me catch my breath and be inspired by my God. Amen.

Heart Treasure: In Jesus, I find the balm of the Psalms.

Finding Your Morning Strength

In the early morning, while it was still dark, Jesus got up,
left the house and went off to a deserted place, and there he prayed.
MARK 1:35 PHILLIPS

*D*id you ever have one of those mornings, around ten or eleven o'clock, when you felt unfocused, uncreative, vulnerable, defenseless, and weak? Did you miss breakfast—or even worse, skip prayer?

Perhaps the day started at breakneck speed. Maybe the baby started crying and you had to roll out of bed at the crack of dawn to change a diaper or grab a bottle. Maybe you got an early-morning phone call that rocked your world. Or maybe you simply overslept.

But there's always time for prayer. Even short and simple ones, ones that take your focus away from yourself and onto God. Ones that give you the equipment, the tools, the power to face the day ahead. Ones that you can say while you're holding a crying infant or before you pick up that phone. Ones you can say when you're making breakfast, driving to work, or heading to a meeting.

Whenever your morning starts, wherever you are, whoever is with you, pray. Whether you have the time to get away, while it's dark, and go off to a place alone to pray or you are saying a prayer on the run, pray. Get yourself out of yourself and into God. Allow Him to provide you with what you need.

Isaiah 33:2 (AMPC) gives you a good place to start: "O Lord, be gracious to us; we have waited [expectantly] for You. Be the arm [of Your servants—their strength and defense] every morning, our salvation in the time of trouble." To get more out of this verse, consider personalizing it, praying, "O Lord, be gracious to *me*; *I* have waited expectantly for You. Be *my* arm, the arm of Your servant—*my* strength and defense every morning, *my* rescuer in times of trouble."

To make this prayer even more effective, add physical motions when you say it. Perhaps lift your arms and look to the heavens when you say, "O Lord." Open them wide when you say, "I have waited expectantly for You." Hold your arms firm and at your side when you say, "Be my arm, the arm of Your servant." Move your arms into weight-lifting position when you say, "My strength." Then swing them so they protect your face as you say, "And defense every morning." Finally, bring them down and relax them as you slowly look up and say, "My rescuer in times of trouble."

However, whenever, wherever, and whatever you decide to pray in the morning (consider Psalm 59:16; 73:26; 86:2; 143:8), just do it. It's the most important part of your day.

Thank You, Jesus, for hearing my prayer. Help me to be like You and seek Father God at the beginning of every day.

Heart Treasure: In Jesus, I find my morning strength.

Finding God's Wisdom and Blessing

*He who leans on, trusts in, and is confident of his own mind
and heart is a [self-confident] fool, but he who walks in
skillful and godly Wisdom shall be delivered.*

PROVERBS 28:26 AMPC

*Y*ou haven't had a chance to send your sister a card. So you call her on her birthday, but she doesn't pick up the phone. When the phone beeps, you leave your somewhat off-key rendition of "Happy Birthday" on her voice mail, adding, "Hope you have a good day!" and hang up. The minutes tick by. No response.

Then your imagination kicks in. Maybe she's mad. Upset that you didn't even find time to mail her a card. If you had, she'd have it by now!

All the sweet backstory you share with her turns into resentment of the times she did this or that. Next thing you know you're angry! *The nerve of her! Really! So I was late with a card. The least she could do is return my call!*

Or you read a friend's post on Facebook, and not hearing her tone of voice or knowing her mood, you take offense. You're hurt. *How could she have said that!*

Or your husband doesn't notice your new do. *He hates my hair, I just know it! Maybe he's tired of me!*

"Oh, the thinks you can think!" writes Dr. Seuss, encouraging children to use their imaginations. Yet sometimes, especially as adults, the things we can think lead us astray. Due to misunderstandings, mis-thinkings, our imaginations take a wrong turn, leaving us anxious or angry, sending us off the mental deep end.

But then you find out your sister was sick, and that's why she didn't call back! Or your friend's post meant something totally different than you thought! Or your husband, earlier preoccupied by work, now tells you you're gorgeous!

What a lot of time you've wasted, not to mention the anxiety you suffered thinking what you thought!

Proverbs 28:26 says not to be confident of the things you think but to seek, walk in, and live by God's wisdom. As Peter says, Christians are to have "no retaliation. No sharp-tongued sarcasm. Instead, bless—that's your job, to bless. You'll be a blessing and also get a blessing" (1 Peter 3:9 MSG).

So the next time you feel hurt, injured, or ignored, don't get anxious or angry because of what you *think* is happening. Stick with God's wisdom. Give others the benefit of the doubt. Even better, bless them no matter what. For then not only will your anxiety and anger fade, but you yourself will be blessed.

Lord Jesus, help me to rely on God's wisdom, not my own vain imaginings about what's going on with other people. Help me to do as You did and continue to do: be a blessing! In Your name I pray, amen.

Heart Treasure: In Jesus, I find God's wisdom and blessing.

Finding Heart-Filled Forgiveness

*At that point Peter got up the nerve to ask, "Master, how many
times do I forgive a brother or sister who hurts me? Seven?"
Jesus replied, "Seven! Hardly. Try seventy times seven."*
MATTHEW 18:21–22 MSG

Jesus presented a radical concept of forgiveness for His day. And you
could say it's just as radical in this world we live in today. Most people
live by the eye-for-an-eye edict. Yet Jesus tells us to replace our animalistic
urge for revenge with the heavenly intention to love all!

But back to Jesus' day. . . The *MacArthur Study Bible* footnote to
Matthew 18:21 says that "Peter thought he was being magnanimous.
The rabbis, citing several verses from Amos (1:3, 6, 9, 11, 13) taught that
since God forgave Israel's enemies only 3 times, it was presumptuous and
unnecessary to forgive anyone more than 3 times."

That gives you a bit of the history behind this verse and reveals how
mind-blowing was Jesus' response of "seventy times seven"!

Perhaps you too feel magnanimous when you forgive someone once,
twice, or three times. Depending, of course, on the degree of the infraction,
that's relatively easy to do. But four times, five times, or more! How can
you ever do it!

Instead of thinking about forgiving the person, we're more likely to say
to ourselves, "Really? Again? How many times do I have to tell her not to
do that? When will she ever learn?" That opens the door to the woe-is-me
syndrome. Or, worse, the I'm-not-going-to-take-this-anymore mind-set,
leading to anger, resentment, and perhaps revenge.

Yet Jesus would have us take another tack. If someone slaps us on the
face, He wants us to offer the other cheek. Or if someone steals our coat,
to give them our shirt as well.

Why? Why, oh, why does Jesus call us to respond this way? Because that's how God treats us! When we sin, He forgives us over and over again. Certainly more than 490 times! When it comes to debts, He forgives those too! For how could we ever repay Him for what Jesus has done for us?

So we are called not just to forgive those who mistreat us but to bless them!

And how are we to do it? From the heart. Because our Father is constantly doing it for us! And if we don't forgive others? God won't forgive us (Matthew 18:35).

Forgiving others seems like a tall order, Jesus, but I know that with God I can do anything. So help me forgive others, even if I have to do it over and over again. Give me Your patience to do what You call me to do. And may I do it with Your power filling my heart.

Heart Treasure: In Jesus, I find heart-filled forgiveness.

....

....

....

....

....

....

....

....

....

....

....

Finding Your True Shield and Great Reward

After these things, the word of the Lord came to Abram in a vision, saying, Fear not, Abram, I am your Shield, your abundant compensation, and your reward shall be exceedingly great.

GENESIS 15:1 AMPC

We work, we scrimp, we save, we worry how we will make ends meet. How will we provide for, defend, and protect our loved ones? And what will be our reward?

In Genesis 14, we read how Abraham discovered that his kinsmen (including his nephew Lot residing in Sodom) and all their goods were taken captive by some warring kings. So Abraham led his warriors out at night and "recovered all the goods that had been taken, and he brought back his nephew Lot with his possessions and all the women and other captives" (Genesis 14:16 NLT).

When the king of Sodom offered Abraham a reward, he refused, saying, "I solemnly swear to the LORD, God Most High, Creator of heaven and earth, that I will not take so much as a single thread or sandal thong from what belongs to you. Otherwise you might say, 'I am the one who made Abram rich'" (Genesis 14:22–23 NLT). Abraham accepted only what his men had already eaten and requested only that the kings who had battled with him get their fair share of spoils. Immediately after that, the Lord told Abraham, "Fear not. . .I am your Shield. . .and your reward shall be exceedingly great" (Genesis 15:1 AMPC).

You, as a believer in Jesus Christ, are a child of God, a seed of Abraham (Galatians 3:29). And as with Abraham, God has promised to be your shield and reward. Now, most of us don't own a shield or know much about the way a shield might be used in battle. But we're familiar with the windshields on our cars. Those shields are usually made of safety glass, protecting us from the wind, dirt, rocks, insects, and debris as we drive along.

Well, God is even better than a windshield, saving us from things flying our way. When we trust in Him, instead of in money or the help of our fellow human beings, God not only shields us but becomes our "abundant compensation," our great reward. For when we look to Him for all, we receive all we need—and more!

To get on Abraham's wavelength, agree with Paul, who wrote, "Everything else is worthless when compared with the infinite value of knowing Christ Jesus my Lord" (Philippians 3:8 NLT). Make God alone your shield and exceedingly great reward, giving Him all the credit for what you have and who you are, and all your fears will fade.

Help me, Jesus, to look only to Father God for protection and provision. For when I do, I know I will be greatly rewarded. Praise Your name! Amen.

Heart Treasure: In Jesus, I find my true shield and great reward.

Finding the Best Plan

What we read in Scripture is, "Abraham entered into what God was doing for him, and that was the turning point. He trusted God to set him right instead of trying to be right on his own."
ROMANS 4:3 MSG

God tells us He's our shield and great reward (Genesis 15:1). Thus, we need not be afraid. With Him in our camp, on our side, going before us and keeping us safe, we'll lack nothing. That's what He told Abraham. And that's what He tells us.

But then, as with Abraham, our response may begin with, "What will you give me. . ." (Genesis 15:2 ESV) and end with, ". . .because here's what I lack." Following that would most likely be our own solution to our problem. That's how Abraham's conversation with God unfolded. He told God he lacked a child, a son. So he figured a member of his household, perhaps a slave, would be his heir. That's when God set Abraham straight, telling him that his very own son would be his heir and that Abraham's descendants would be more numerable than the stars in the heavens. The next verse reads, "And he [Abram] believed in (trusted in, relied on, remained steadfast to) the Lord, and He counted it to him as righteousness (right standing with God)" (Genesis 15:6 AMPC).

Oh, that we would have such faith! That we would go to God and tell Him what we want, wish for, dream of—and then be patient enough to wait for Him to respond.

The problem, of course, is that it's easy to get impatient, to take things into our own hands. We have a need, come up with an idea, and then plan how to implement it to bring about what we desire. And then we're surprised when it all blows up in our face!

That's kind of what happened to Abraham's wife, Sarah. When she lost her patience waiting for their promised son, she came up with an alternative plan. She gave Abraham her slave Hagar, and Ishmael was born. But that wasn't God's plan at all! And the entire deal blew up in their faces—and continues to have repercussions today in the Middle East! If only Sarah would have been patient and trusted God enough to wait for her son Isaac, how different the world would be.

The point is to trust Jesus—God's Son and Abraham's descendant. Rise above your impatience by truly believing God has a much better plan for your life than you could ever imagine. Enter into what God is doing for you. Trust God to set you right.

Lord Jesus, I often get impatient with God's timing. Help me to look to Him for all my guidance, to trust that He has the best plan. And so I wait on Him, confident He'll more than match my dreams.

Heart Treasure: In Jesus, I find the best plan.

Finding the Everlasting Arms

*It was a case of Christ's strength moving in on my weakness. Now I take
limitations in stride, and with good cheer, these limitations that cut me
down to size—abuse, accidents, opposition, bad breaks. I just let Christ
take over! And so the weaker I get, the stronger I become.*
2 CORINTHIANS 12:9–10 MSG

*Y*ou have an illness you can't seem to shake. Then, finally back on your
feet, you return to work, only to be abused by your boss's comments
about using up too much sick time. The next morning, while taking the
dog for a walk, you trip on the sidewalk and break your elbow. After being
fitted with a sling and a splint, you get home and your husband asks who's
going to be cooking the meals if you can't even hold a pot.

You get the idea. Some days we wonder why we even get out of bed.
Then sometimes those days turn into weeks. We get low, keep falling down,
down, down, wondering if we'll ever reach the bottom.

But there is hope. You have a place to go, Someone who will help you,
Someone with more power than you'll ever hope to have. Moses pointed it
out way back in Deuteronomy. He was blessing the Israelites, giving them
a good word in his last days, knowing he would never see the Promised
Land: "The eternal God is your refuge and dwelling place, and underneath
are the everlasting arms" (Deuteronomy 33:27 AMPC).

There is no low you can sink to where God is unable to hold, boost, lift
you up. All you need to do is make Him your refuge. When you do, Christ
will be there with His strength that will move in on your weakness. When
you let Him take over during those days of bad breaks, you learn to take
all that happens not just in stride but cheerfully!

The psalmist can help you get there by giving you a good visual: "GOD's
my island hideaway, keeps danger far from the shore, throws garlands of
hosannas around my neck" (Psalm 32:7 MSG). And once you spend some
time in your Refuge, once you consider the many blessings you've received,

you can start giving yourself some grace talks: "I said to myself, 'Relax and rest. GOD has showered you with blessings. Soul, you've been rescued from death; Eye, you've been rescued from tears; and you, Foot, were kept from stumbling' " (Psalm 116:7–8 MSG).

Allow God's Word and Jesus' grace to lift you up.

Jesus, in You I find the everlasting arms of grace and strength. As I abide in You, as I make You the place where I dwell, I know I'll never be down for long. So, soul and spirit, relax and rest. God's got it covered. Amen.

Heart Treasure: In Jesus, I find the everlasting arms of grace and strength.

Finding the Worthy Road

*"Now get up and stand on your feet for I have shown myself to you for
a reason—you are chosen to be my servant and a witness to
what you have seen of me today, and of other visions of
myself which I will give you. I will keep you safe."*

ACTS 26:16–17 PHILLIPS

God has a plan for your life. But perhaps you aren't following it because you don't feel able or good enough to do as He wills. Maybe you feel unworthy. Perhaps you have a shady past—or present. Or maybe you think God hasn't yet told you His will for your life.

Consider Saul. Before he became the apostle Paul, Saul was persecuting the people of the new Way—Jesus' Way. But while he was traveling the road to Damascus, Jesus made it blindingly clear that Saul was *not* walking in the right direction. In fact, He asked Saul why he was persecuting Him. Then Jesus said, "It is useless for you to fight against my will" (Acts 26:14 NLT). Some Bibles translate this as "kicking against the goads [to keep offering vain and perilous resistance]" (AMPC) or "going against the grain" (MSG) or "kick[ing] against your own conscience" (PHILLIPS). But it all boils down to the same thing: you can't fight God's will or Jesus' purpose for your life.

It's time for you to rise up, stand on your feet. Jesus has shown Himself to you for a reason. You're His servant. He's going to give you a plan, and as you carry it out, He promises you His safety and protection, His strength and power, His provision and forgiveness. Yes, forgiveness.

Jesus was human once. He knows the things you face. Although He never once gave in to temptation, He knows the struggle against it.

So be assured. You *are* good enough. God *does* have a plan for your life. Stop resisting His will. Get in line with Jesus' purpose for you. Arise, stand on your feet, and start walking down His path. If you take a wrong turn, He'll set you back on the right road.

In regard to your past missteps, ask Jesus for His forgiveness. Pray with the psalmist, "Do not remember against me my former iniquities; let your compassion come speedily to meet me" (see Psalm 79:8 ESV). When you do, Jesus will rain down His love and mercy. Then the only thing remaining for you will be to follow God's plan. And your way will be the Way.

Lord, I want to take the path You have planned for me to walk.
Let Your compassions come down speedily to meet me, to take away
the unworthiness I feel. Forgive me of those things that weigh me down,
that keep me from rising up in You. In Jesus' name I pray, amen.

Heart Treasure: In Jesus, I find the worthy road.

Finding Faith That God's Will Is Right

Jesus said to her, Did I not tell you and promise you that if you would believe and rely on Me, you would see the glory of God?
JOHN 11:40 AMPC

ou see no way out of your present circumstances. You've tried a number of different solutions, thinking they were the right ones to remedy the problem. But none of them worked. It seems an impossible situation! What's a woman to do?

Trust that God will find a way. That what you think is impossible will be to Him more than possible. Believe He will find a way where you see none!

Max Lucado writes, "Faith is not the belief that God will do what you want. It is the belief that God will do what is right." Do you believe that God will do what's right? Even if that's not really what you'd like to have happen? That can be tough. Especially in cases involving a loved one, when that person's life or earthly future hangs in the balance.

God may do the miraculous. Or He may not. He may heal or He may let die. He may speak loudly and clearly or He may remain silent for a while, longer than you'd like.

When Mary and Martha sent word to Jesus that their brother Lazarus was sick, they most likely expected Him to come on the run. But He didn't. He just said that Lazarus's sickness would not end in death but would glorify and honor God. Then Jesus stayed *two days longer* where He was!

It wasn't that Jesus didn't love this trio of siblings. He did! It wasn't that they hadn't served Jesus. They had! Martha threw Him a dinner party, and Mary anointed His feet with perfume, wiping it up with her hair!

Yet Jesus still delayed His arrival. And by the time He got to their village, Lazarus had died! They knew if Jesus had been there, He could have healed Lazarus. And Jesus was devastated at their grief. Even *He* wept tears of sorrow (John 11:35).

But the story ends happily. Jesus raised Lazarus from the dead. And because of this feat, many glorified God and began believing in Jesus!

The point is to have faith. Trust that Jesus has the best solution. That what may seem impossible to others—including you—is possible with God. And when He has had His way—the right way—all that will be left for you to do is to glorify Him!

I can't see how this situation is going to turn out right, Lord, but I know whatever way You choose will be the right way. Build up my faith and trust in You so I can cling to the hope that is only available with You. And as You work out Your will, may You get all the glory. In Jesus' sweet name I pray, amen.

Heart Treasure: In Jesus, I find the faith that God's will is right.

Finding the Anchor for Your Soul

We who have run for our very lives to God have every reason to grab the promised hope with both hands and never let go. It's an unbreakable spiritual lifeline, reaching past all appearances right to the very presence of God where Jesus, running on ahead of us, has taken up his permanent post as high priest for us.

HEBREWS 6:18–20 MSG

We like to hold on to things, things from our past. Throughout the seasons of our lives, we've had things that have given us comfort as we cried. There's the tearstained teddy bear from our childhood that now sits on a shelf, just in case we need him. Our grandmother's afghan, the colors now out of style and somewhat faded, is draped over the back of our favorite chair. Dad's old tackle box sits covered with dust in the garage. An aunt's wooden spoon holder adorns a kitchen wall. Our mother-in-law's big pasta pot is shoved to the back of our kitchen cabinet. The tiny undershirt our now-grown child once wore lies buried deep in our sock drawer. Photos, in albums and cluttering the memory on our cell phone, are brought out and looked at.

These are things we look to when we feel lost, untethered, unsure. They warm our hearts, give us comfort, remind us that no matter what happens, all will be well. These things that people have left behind remind us of how they once loved us.

Jesus has also left things behind, including a hope to hold on to "with both hands" to "never let go." It's the hope that because of His life and sacrifice, we have unending access to God. No matter what storms we go through, no matter where, when, or why we cry, our Abba God is there to hold us.

Along with this hope, Jesus sent the Holy Spirit to comfort us, to lead us. With Him in our lives, we know we are never truly alone, never truly lost.

And Jesus left us God's Word. When the rains come pouring down, within or without, we have something to turn to. We find the relief, the solace, the courage, the renewal, the nourishment we need for what God has called us to do and be in this life.

So when you need hope, guidance, comfort, a friend—look to Jesus, reach out to the Spirit, and linger in God's Word, knowing that in these treasures you will find your way to face another day. Never let them go.

I'm looking to You, Jesus, for hope. To the Spirit for comfort and guidance. To God's Word for the nourishment I need to live this life for You. And I'm never letting go. In Jesus' name, amen.

Heart Treasure: In Jesus, I find the anchor for my soul.

Finding the Nurturing You Need

*He will feed his flock like a shepherd. He will carry the lambs
in his arms, holding them close to his heart. He will gently
lead the mother sheep with their young.*

Isaiah 40:11 NLT

Have you ever had one of those mornings, days, weeks, months, years when you can't remember the last time you heard a thank-you? When everyone has been pulling at you, wanting or needing something they say only you can provide?

Where does the nurturer go to be nurtured? Where does the cook go to be fed? Where does the mother sheep go to find guidance and direction? She might try going to a family member—a father, mother, sister, or brother. Perhaps a friend or her pastor. Maybe she even has a mentor.

Such people might replenish you in some way, nourish you. They might even have some great advice. But there's a better resource, One with amazing vision and perception. One who can give "ewe" just what you need.

His name is Jesus. He's the Good Shepherd (John 10:11). And He's not just your Good Shepherd, there to feed, carry, and guide you. He's also your spiritual Brother (Hebrews 2:11; Romans 8:29; Mark 3:34–35) because you're a child of God.

It gets even better. Because you believe in Jesus, you have access to Father God, who also has mothering characteristics! Here are some verses that reveal the many sides of His motherly nature:

- *He comforts:* "I will comfort you. . .as a mother comforts her child" (Isaiah 66:13 NLT).
- *He loves and remembers:* "Can a mother forget her nursing child? Can she feel no love for the child she has borne? But even if that were possible, I would not forget you!" (Isaiah 49:15 NLT).
- *He defends like a lioness:* "Like a bear whose cubs have been taken

away, I will tear out your heart. I will devour you like a hungry lioness and mangle you like a wild animal" (Hosea 13:8 NLT).

- *He carries you on His wings:* "Like an eagle that rouses her chicks and hovers over her young, so he spread his wings to take them up and carried them safely on his pinions" (Deuteronomy 32:11 NLT).

Do you need some nurturing, feeding, guidance, direction, and so much more? Need a supernatural dose of good advice? Spend some time with Brother Jesus, Father God, and the Word. They'll give you exactly what you need in this world—and the next.

> *Brother Jesus, You are just what I need today. Fill me with Your presence. Lead me to Father God. Give me the nurturing I need to empower me to meet the needs of others. Amen.*

Heart Treasure: In Jesus, I find the nurturing I need.

Finding the Nearness of God

Draw near to God, and he will draw near to you.
JAMES 4:8 ESV

*H*ave you been outrageously busy lately? Do you feel like your life is careening out of control? Do you wonder what's happened to God, why He's not helping you get a handle on it? Maybe He's wondering what's happened to you!

Jesus tells us in Matthew 22:37–38 (MSG), " 'Love the Lord your God with all your passion and prayer and intelligence.' This is the most important, the first on any list." Hmm. Is spending time with God the first thing on *your* daily to-do list? If not, that may be why your life feels like it's gone haywire.

James 4:8 says that if we draw near to God, He'll draw near to us. But that doesn't mean saying a quick help-me-Lord prayer in the morning and thinking that will carry you throughout the entire day. Nor does it mean saying the same long prayer every morning and ignoring God the rest of the day. Doing those things day after day will make you poorly equipped to handle the real-life challenges that are bound to come along (Isaiah 29:13–14).

Drawing near to God means having an intimate relationship with Him. It involves slowing down, getting on His timetable, digging deep into His Word, and engaging in heart-to-heart communion with Him. God wants to spend time with you. And when you do, you'll quickly realize the benefits (Psalm 73:28).

Jesus has given you the avenue to come boldly to God, to approach His throne. For it's there you'll receive His mercy and grace to lift you up (Hebrews 4:16; 7:19). Don't rebuff that access by ignoring it, being too busy, turning your back on God. Instead, turn the other way—to God. And do so with confidence, knowing Jesus has paved the way (Hebrews 10:22).

Perhaps it's time you have a heart-to-heart with God. Draw near to Him just to be near Him. Can't find the words to say? No worries. Just go. Be silent before Him, asking for nothing, just being in His presence.

Or go to the Psalms for words to quench your thirst, prime your soul, meditate on, or pray back to God. Try using the words of King David's love letter to God: "My heart has heard you say, 'Come and talk with me.' And my heart responds, 'LORD, I am coming' " (Psalm 27:8 NLT).

The point is to go to God. Draw near to your Maker and Creator. And He'll draw near to you.

Jesus, thank You for giving me access to the Father, for being my doorway to God's presence. Lead me into a heart-to-heart meeting with my Creator. In Your name I pray, amen.

Heart Treasure: In Jesus, I find the nearness of God.

Finding Your Open Door

"I've opened a door before you that no one can slam shut. You don't have much strength, I know that; you used what you had to keep my Word."
REVELATION 3:8 MSG

*D*ecisions come in various sizes. Some are big, some small, some seemingly inconsequential. We make them every day based on our current knowledge. And so they *seem* like they're good decisions. . .at the time.

Then one day, you're at the grocery store checkout counter. You hear the cashier give you the total. You look into your wallet and begin counting out the cash. Your heart sinks as you realize that after paying this grocery bill, you'll have barely enough to get through the rest of the week. Your mind starts wondering, *How is this possible? I thought I'd be a lot further along at this point in my life, that making ends meet wouldn't be such a struggle anymore.* And hopelessness starts to set in.

You begin thinking about all the decisions you made in the past, from the distant days (the course you chose in school) to the more recent one (the sirloin you selected instead of the chuck roast that's on sale). *Maybe I haven't made the right decisions all along.*

From that sense of hopelessness comes doubt, discouragement, distraction. Your mind, now consumed with what-might-have-beens, births feelings of dissatisfaction with your current lot. You begin looking down and out, instead of up and in.

Don't get caught up in the whirlpool of despair that circles endlessly and drags you down into its depths. Thank God for the blessings that have come into your life. For God doesn't want you so fixated on the past that you miss what He's doing in the present and has planned for your future (Jeremiah 29:11–13; Philippians 3:13–14; Isaiah 43:18).

Hear the words of Jesus saying, "I know all the things you do, and I have opened a door for you that no one can close. You have little strength, yet you obeyed my word and did not deny me" (Revelation 3:8 NLT).

And when it comes to decisions, big or small, let God in. Open your ears. He'll steer you in the right direction, point out the path He wants you to take: "Your own ears will hear him. Right behind you a voice will say, 'This is the way you should go,' whether to the right or to the left" (Isaiah 30:21 NLT).

I'm not sure how I got here, Lord, but I know You're with me every step of the way. May I consult You with every decision I have to make. Help me to keep my ears open so I can hear Your voice giving me directions. I want to make the right turns and praise Your name no matter where I end up. My hope lies in finding Your open door!

Heart Treasure: In Jesus, I find my open door.

Finding Peace with Button Pushers

"Love your neighbor as yourself."
MATTHEW 22:39 NLT

*M*ost of us are familiar with the student of religion who asked Jesus what the most important of the Ten Commandments was. Jesus told him the greatest rule is to love God with all our being. And that the second rule, to love our neighbors as we do ourselves, is just as important.

So we think, *Okay. I'll really love God. And I'll love everyone I come in contact with as much as I love myself.* And we feel pretty good about that. With our friends and loved ones, it seems actually doable. And then we encounter someone who just constantly pushes our buttons. We're walking along, whistling a happy I-can-do-this tune, until we see that face. The face of the one who's argumentative, disruptive, insulting, and everything we hope we aren't. And our heart sinks down to the pit of our stomach. We think back to all the things this person has said or done in the past. And suddenly loving him is the last thing on our mind.

But Jesus didn't say to love just your friends and most family members. He said you're to love even your enemies. And perhaps this button pusher seems like an enemy. After all, you react to him physically as if he were. But God would have you *love* that button pusher, to bless him if he curses you, to pray for him if he hurts you, and more (Luke 6:27–31).

Regardless of whether this person is friend, family, or foe, you need to handle the situation. But you can't do it alone. You need to call on all the powers of God. You need to remember that you're not to "think you are better than you really are," but that you're to "be honest in your evaluation" of yourself (Romans 12:3 NLT). Perhaps some people think *you're* a difficult person at times. Hmm. That's food for thought!

So what can you do when facing someone who seems like an enemy? Instead of running from the challenge before you, go to God. Ask Him to calm your heart. To make you humble. To give you the words He wants you to say—or to help you remain silent. To be patient. To give love and kindness without expecting any in return. And most importantly, to pray for that person. When you're with him and when you're not. Pray for blessings to rain down upon him. In that way, no matter whom you meet, you'll be taken up with God's loving-kindness instead of brought down by your emotions as you leave all in His good hands.

Sometimes, Jesus, I want to run when I encounter specific button pushers. But I'm here now, before You, praying for You to bless each one. Help me remember that we all come to You imperfect. Hold the button pushers and me in Your good hands. Amen.

Heart Treasure: In Jesus, I find peace with button pushers.

....

....

....

....

....

....

....

....

....

....

....

Finding How to Take Heart

*"Yet now I urge you to take heart. . . . For this very night there stood
before me an angel of the God to whom I belong and whom I worship,
and he said, 'Do not be afraid. . . .' So take heart, men, for I have
faith in God that it will be exactly as I have been told."*
Acts 27:22–25 esv

Those are Paul's words. He and his shipmates were in a boatload of
trouble. But an angel of God came and told him not to be afraid.
Although the ship would be lost in the storm, no man's life would. So
Paul encouraged his shipmates with these words, telling them to "take
heart"—because he believed God's promise to him.

Jesus tells us in John 16:33 to take heart and not worry, because
although we may see trouble, He has overcome the world.

To "take heart" means to be encouraged, to regain your courage. To
know that although things may look bleak, everything will turn out fine.

So how can we do this when we're feeling discouraged and hopeless
and no angel appears? When we're in the midst of the storm and our ship
is breaking up? When we've done all we can do and still see no clear sky
on the horizon?

That's when we must have faith in God and Jesus, faith in the promises
our Father and Brother have given us.

Take to heart the words of Psalm 31:24 (ampc): "Be strong and let
your heart take courage, all you who wait for and hope for and expect
the Lord!" And Psalm 27:14 (ampc): "Wait and hope for and expect the
Lord; be brave and of good courage and let your heart be stout and
enduring. Yes, wait for and hope for and expect the Lord." Take to mind
Psalm 27:13 (esv) by memorizing every word: "I believe that I shall look
upon the goodness of the Lord in the land of the living!" Being able to
call up this verse in the face of stormy weather will ensure you stay afloat
no matter what comes your way.

All of God's promises were written to help you stay above the fray, out of the darkness that discouragement can bring. But you must know them and have faith that what God says He'll do, He. . .will. . .do.

Help me, Lord Jesus, to take heart when trouble comes my way. To know that God will come through on His promises. Change my mind-set from one of discouragement to encouragement. And help me to encourage others along the way. In Your name I pray, amen.

Heart Treasure: In Jesus, I find how to take heart.

Finding True Friends

"When two of you get together on anything at all on earth and make a prayer of it, my Father in heaven goes into action. And when two or three of you are together because of me, you can be sure that I'll be there."
MATTHEW 18:19–20 MSG

*Y*ou may encounter times when you feel so weak, you have trouble finding your way to Jesus. That's when your fellow believers can help carry you there.

It happened to a paraplegic. His four friends heard that Jesus was in someone's house. They carried the man there, but the crowd outside made it impossible for them to even get near the door. Determined to get this man to the Healer, they removed part of the roof and lowered the man and his bed through the opening!

The Bible says, "When Jesus saw their faith, he said to the man on the bed, 'My son, your sins are forgiven' " (Mark 2:5 PHILLIPS). Of course, the scribes hearing these words started thinking, *Who does this Jesus think He is? Only God can forgive sins.* Jesus, who can read men's thoughts, said, "Just so you know that I, the Son of Man, can both forgive sins and heal, that I can do one, the other, or both. . ." He paused then turned to the paraplegic and said, "Get up, pick up your bed, and go home" (see Mark 2:11). And the man immediately did, causing the crowd to gape in amazement and give glory to God!

Talk about the determination of faith-filled friends! Talk about faith, Jesus, and God in action!

Whether you're sin-sick, soul-sick, or spiritually sick, Jesus can heal you. And if you're so sick you can't seem to make your way to His side, be humble enough to confide in a few friends, ones who have taken to heart Jesus' commandment: "Love each other in the same way I have loved you" (John 15:12 NLT). For they are the friends who will allow no obstacle to stand between you and your making your way to Jesus. No crowds, no roofs, no naysayers can impede their determination to see you healed of whatever's keeping you down.

And when you're not weak, when you're able to aid another who cannot get up, help that person make her way through to the One who calls you friend. For Jesus has said, "You are my friends when you do the things I command you. I'm no longer calling you servants because servants don't understand what their master is thinking and planning. No, I've named you friends because I've let you in on everything I've heard from the Father" (John 15:14–15 MSG).

*Lord Jesus, thank You for friends who help me when I'm so weak
I cannot make my way to You. And when I am well, help me to
be such a friend as they. In Jesus' name I pray, amen.*

Heart Treasure: In Jesus, I find true friends.

Finding the Straight Path

Lean on, trust in, and be confident in the Lord with all your heart and mind and do not rely on your own insight or understanding. In all your ways know, recognize, and acknowledge Him, and He will direct and make straight and plain your paths.
PROVERBS 3:5–6 AMPC

Who's in control of your life? You or God?

Some people say God is their copilot. Hmm. Then He's not really in control of the plane, is He? Others say to put God in the driver's seat. That sounds a little more like what God had in mind.

Yet sometimes it can be difficult to be in the passenger seat when someone else is driving the car. When a traffic light is yellow and the driver doesn't even begin to slow down, you may find your foot reaching for a nonexistent brake on your side of the car. Or you find yourself unable to *not* tell the driver the best way to reach your destination. And when she doesn't take *your* route, you can't help but issue a *tsk* from your lips and shake your head at her naïveté.

Yes, it's difficult to rely on and put your trust in a human driver. But God isn't human. He's supernatural, all-powerful, all-knowing, and all-wise. He gives you instructions to live by in His Book. And His Son, Jesus, vouches for Him and the benefits you'll gain by following Him, saying, "Blessed (happy and to be envied) rather are those who hear the Word of God and obey and practice it!" (Luke 11:28 AMPC).

Perhaps it's time to unclench your white-knuckled fists from the steering wheel of your life. Maybe you actually need to get out of that driver's seat and into the passenger seat in *all* areas, not just some. Perhaps it's time to trust God with all of you, from the tips of your brake-seeking toes to the top of your shaking head.

For when you allow God to be in control of your life, when you trust

Him with all your heart and mind, when you leave the driving to Him and allow His wisdom and instincts to override your own, only then can you begin to relax and really live. Because you know that you're exactly where He wants you to be. And that He'll get you exactly where He wants you to go.

I know I'm to give God full control over my life, Lord Jesus. Help me to build up my trust in Him. To realize I can relax being the passenger when He's in the driver's seat. As I seek His will in all things, I know I'll be on the right path to Him. In Jesus' name I pray, amen.

Heart Treasure: In Jesus, I find the straight path.

Finding Your Real Life

I am trusting you. Show me where to walk, for I give myself to you.
PSALM 143:8 NLT

ou wake up full of energy. You have a plan for your day, know exactly what you'll be doing when and where. And then you get a text. Your daughter has a chance to get in some overtime at work if you can pick up your granddaughter from day care that evening. Or you get a phone call. Your Realtor has someone who wants to see your house; can you have things looking nice and be out by eleven this morning? Or you get an email from your pastor, asking if you can put the prayer chain through.

So much for the day you had so perfectly planned. Frustrated, you say yes to the request. But your heart isn't in it—at all. Or, even worse, you say no and then spend the rest of the day feeling selfish or guilty.

Jesus experienced a lot of interruptions. In Matthew 14, He hears that His cousin John the Baptist has been beheaded. "As soon as Jesus heard the news, he left in a boat to a remote area to be alone" (Matthew 14:13 NLT). Sounds reasonable. Yet then we read the rest of the verse: "But the crowds heard where he was headed and followed on foot."

Can you imagine? He's trying to get some peace and quiet, some time away from everyone, yet they follow Him! The nerve! Yet "Jesus saw the huge crowd as he stepped from the boat, and he had compassion on them and healed their sick" (verse 14 NLT). From there He went on to feed over five thousand people, then walked on water!

Earlier, in Matthew 9, *while* preaching, Jesus is interrupted by a man whose daughter has just died. He asks Jesus to come with him to bring her back to life. On the way, a hemorrhaging woman pushes through the crowd to touch Him. Jesus stops and has a conversation with her. After healing her, He reaches the girl and brings her back to life, and as He's leaving her home, two blind men ask for mercy and healing. Talk about interruptions!

You may have a plan. But God and His plan have priority over yours. C. S. Lewis wrote, "The truth is of course that what one calls the interruptions are precisely one's real life—the life God is sending one day by day: what one calls one's 'real life' is a phantom of one's own imagination!"

The next time you're interrupted, have compassion. Let go of your imaginary "real life," and live joyfully the life God has sent you.

Here's my day, Jesus. I put it in Your hands. Help me to have compassion when I'm interrupted, to embrace the "real life" You send my way, knowing You're the one who's truly in control. "Show me where to walk, for I give myself to you."

Heart Treasure: In Jesus, I find my real life.

Finding Enough

*Let your character or moral disposition be free from love of money
[including greed, avarice, lust, and craving for earthly possessions]
and be satisfied with your present [circumstances and with what you
have]; for He [God] Himself has said, I will not in any way fail you nor
give you up nor leave you without support. [I will] not, [I will] not,
[I will] not in any degree leave you helpless nor forsake nor
let [you] down (relax My hold on you)! [Assuredly not!]*
HEBREWS 13:5 AMPC

You started out your life with hopes and dreams and the energy to realize them. And then the years passed. Suddenly it hits you. Life didn't turn out at all like you'd imagined.

Perhaps you modeled yourself after your parents, thinking you'd be able to retire when they did. And you're nowhere near that. In fact, you figure you'll have to work until the day you die! Or maybe you're not in that place at all. Maybe you're more than financially set for the rest of your days. Yet that dream you'd had as a child has somehow been lost. In fact, you're not even sure you can remember what you wanted to do or be.

Here's the thing. No matter what's going on in your life, no matter where you are (or aren't), God wants you to be satisfied with where you've landed, to be content with what you have, not bemoaning what could've been or what you think should've been.

Remember the Israelites wandering in the wilderness? God continually rescued and provided for them. He led them out of slavery. He provided them with manna. He led them to water in a parched land. But still they were not satisfied. They constantly complained, grumbling beneath their breath and crying, "More! More! More!"

God doesn't want you to be constantly looking at your lack but rather reveling in your blessings. And two of those blessings are Jesus and the Holy Spirit. The first gives you direct access—anytime and anywhere—to

God; He's the Man who worked God's plan. The second is the One who convinces you of God's truths.

And, of course, you have the blessings of Father God. He will in no way fail to make good on His promises to you. He'll never leave you without support. And, as the *Amplified Bible* asserts three times, He will not, will not, will not ever, in any way, leave you helpless or alone. He will never, never, never relax His grip on you.

Dig deep into this idea of having and being more than enough. Allow it to lift you up to a joyful life in Christ.

Thank You for the reminder, Lord Jesus, that with You in my life, I have it all! And that no matter what's happening, by the power of Father God and the Holy Spirit, I need not worry but praise. In Jesus' name, amen.

Heart Treasure: In Jesus, I find enough.

Finding God's Peace and Power

Let be and be still, and know (recognize and understand) that I am God.
I will be exalted among the nations! I will be exalted in the earth!
PSALM 46:10 AMPC

*Y*ou're exhausted, trying to do so much in your own power. And you keep hitting wall after wall after wall. So many obstacles have risen up before you; so many things are blocking your way. But God would have you take another path, walk another way.

First, though, God wants you to stop. To be still. To rest your hands, mind, legs, thoughts. To stop trying to do things in your own power. To know that He is God. To open the door to Him who has so much more strength than you could ever summon up. To lift your eyes up to the hills, the heavens, for in God is where your help and strength lie (Psalm 105:4; 121:1–3).

Understand that Jesus, the Son of God within you, has the power to still the wind and the waves, to calm the storms that have risen up. Believe that Jesus will do what He has promised, that He is your ultimate power.

You'll have to begin with your thoughts, the ones crowding out the knowledge that God is your answer, the ones ricocheting in your head saying you'll never meet that deadline, find the words to say, gain the strength to rise.

Remember when Jairus, the leader of the synagogue, came to Jesus to ask Him to heal his dying daughter? As they headed to his house, some messengers came to tell Jairus that his daughter was dead. But Jesus said to him, "Do not be seized with alarm and struck with fear; only keep on believing" (Mark 5:36 AMPC). *The Message* paraphrases this as "Don't listen to them; just trust me." When they arrived at the girl's house, it was filled with mourners weeping and moaning. Before Jesus could do any work, He had to clear the house (Matthew 9:24–25). And then He raised the little girl from the dead!

When you allow God to quell your fears, when you believe in His power and keep on believing, when you trust Him and clear your mind of your anxious thoughts then replace them with God's promises, there's nothing He cannot do through you. And so much better than you could ever do on your own!

So be still, woman. Know that God can do all things. Clear your mind of all that's not of Him. Let go and let God. As you do, God will come through!

Lord Jesus, You and Father God are so much more powerful than I'll ever be. Help me clear my mind of my limited thinking and, in so doing, allow Your thoughts, power, and strength to come through. I believe—and will keep on believing—in You!

Heart Treasure: In Jesus, I find God's peace and power.

Finding and Finishing God's Work

*Jesus said to them, "My food is doing the will of him who
sent me and finishing the work he has given me."*
JOHN 4:34 PHILLIPS

*L*ately it may seem as though your dream is unattainable. Things just aren't falling into place, and you begin to wonder if you'll ever realize it in your life. Discouragement sets in. Your energy starts to flag. And the cloud of not getting what you've been striving for begins to overshadow all other aspects of your life.

King David had a dream—building a house for God. But God had other plans for him. God told him Solomon was to build the temple.

You might think David's response would be, "Really, God? I mean, this was what I'd planned. This was what I thought You wanted me to do! And now You're just going to leave me hanging? I've had enough—I'm out of here!'"

But David was a man after God's own heart. Instead of whining and moaning, instead of turning away from God to some other endeavor, David started to organize and collect the people and materials his son would need to build the temple!

Perhaps you're in a "Really, God?" mode. If so, consider changing things up so God can use you in a more powerful way for a dream more in line with His plans. He can lead you to a new venture if only you will turn and listen to Him and follow His blueprint for your life.

The same wisdom David gave his son can help change up your thoughts: "Know the God of your father and serve him with a whole heart and with a willing mind, for the LORD searches all hearts and understands every plan and thought. If you seek him, he will be found by you" (1 Chronicles 28:9 ESV). God knows what you're thinking, what your plans are. He wants you not just to serve Him wholeheartedly but to have a mind willing to do what He wants you to do. And when you reach out to Him for more information, help, or strength, you'll find it.

Then, when you find out God's new plan for you, "be strong and courageous and do it. Do not be afraid and do not be dismayed, for the Lord God, even my God, is with you. He will not leave you or forsake you, until all the work. . .is finished" (1 Chronicles 28:20 ESV).

Jesus finished God's work for you. Now finish the work God has laid out for you—to the benefit of others and for His glory.

Thank You, Lord, for the plan You have for my life. Give me a willing mind and heart to serve You with my entire being. Help me put aside my own plans and embrace the ones You set up since before time began. I'm ready. What do You want me to do, to finish?

Heart Treasure: In Jesus, I find and finish God's work for me.

Finding Full Dependence on God

"Remain in me, and I will remain in you. For a branch cannot produce fruit if it is severed from the vine, and you cannot be fruitful unless you remain in me. Yes, I am the vine; you are the branches. Those who remain in me, and I in them, will produce much fruit. For apart from me you can do nothing."

JOHN 15:4–5 NLT

Many times we count on things to hold us, lift us up, or keep us secure, but then they fall apart, let us down, fade away to nothing. Or we count on people who end up disappointing us in some way. So we resolve to depend on ourselves alone. We may say things like, "What I've learned is I'm the only person I can really count on."

But God doesn't want us to count on things, others, or ourselves. He wants us to count on Him, to look to Him for all we need, for all our help, for all our courage, for all our triumph. He will never let us down!

Jesus said that unless we remain in Him, depending on Him for all things, we'll bear no fruit. For without Him, we can do nothing.

Remember all the chariots and horses, all the warriors the Egyptian pharaoh took to chase down the fleeing Israelites? God swallowed them up in the Red Sea, the same sea whose waters He parted so that His people could cross over onto dry land!

The psalmist wrote, "Some trust in and boast of chariots and some of horses, but we will trust in and boast of the name of the Lord our God" (Psalm 20:7 AMPC).

So if you're tired of being disappointed by things and people (including yourself), remember Jesus. Know that without Him, you can do nothing. And when you're in dire straits, know that "it is better to take refuge in the LORD than to trust in man. It is better to take refuge in the LORD than to trust in princes" (Psalm 118:8–9 ESV). Then pray with the psalmist, "Out of my distress I called on the LORD; the LORD answered me and set me free.

The LORD is on my side; I will not fear. What can man do to me? The LORD is on my side as my helper" (Psalm 118:5–7 ESV). You will have victory with Jesus at your side—and in your heart and mind.

Oh Lord, I am so tired of being disappointed and discouraged by people and things, including myself. I am looking to depend on You and You alone. Only You can set me free from self-reliance. Only You are a worthy helper, my source of all love, light, power, and strength. It is with You alone I will find the victory! In Jesus' name, amen.

Heart Treasure: In Jesus, I find full dependence on God.

Finding Your Ladder to God

Then he said, "I tell you the truth, you will all see heaven open and the angels of God going up and down on the Son of Man, the one who is the stairway between heaven and earth."

*M*any of us have someone we can count on, someone who has provided for us in the past, to whom we are precious and our welfare is of great concern. Yet when we lose that someone, that mother or father, sister or brother, friend or relation, we can feel as if we're all alone in the world. Yes, we have other friends and relatives, but no one we could rely on to bail us out, lend us money, open their door to us were we to fall into dire straits—no questions asked and only love given!

Jacob might have felt the same way when his brother Esau threatened to kill him, and his father sent him away from the only home he'd ever known.

Jacob traveled many miles, only stopping to rest when the sun went down. Using a stone for a pillow, he lay down to sleep. That's when "he dreamed of a stairway that reached from the earth up to heaven. And he saw the angels of God going up and down the stairway" (Genesis 28:12 NLT). At the top of that stairway was God, who spoke to Jacob, saying, "I am with you, and I will protect you wherever you go. One day I will bring you back to this land. I will not leave you until I have finished giving you everything I have promised you" (verse 15 NLT).

When Jacob awoke from the dream, he said, "Surely the LORD is in this place, and I wasn't even aware of it!" (verse 16 NLT) and claimed that place was "the very gateway to heaven!" (verse 17 NLT).

What God promised to Jacob He promises to you—His presence, protection, and provision. Because of Jesus, God is with you and watching over you. He will make sure all His promises to you are fulfilled. Meanwhile, He has sent angels to help you all along the way!

Your gateway to God is Jesus. He is your stairway to heaven. With Him as your access to Father God, you need never worry or fear that you have been left alone.

Lord Jesus, what a vision! What a dream! Yet I'm making it my reality. You are my ladder to heaven. And angels are constantly going up to heaven and coming down to earth to help me as I live my life for You! Thank You for being my stairway to heaven.

Heart Treasure: In Jesus, I find my ladder to God.

Finding Self-Forgiveness

*Let all that I am praise the L*ORD*; may I never forget the good things*
he does for me. He forgives all my sins and heals all my diseases.
He redeems me from death and crowns me with love and tender mercies.
He fills my life with good things. My youth is renewed like the eagle's!
PSALM 103:2–5 NLT

*D*epending on where your decisions have led you, you may be filled with remorse, regretting what could've been. But being filled with guilt over bad choices or missteps only leads to discouragement and disappointment. Besides, God has forgiven you (Psalm 103:12; Isaiah 43:25). In fact, although He may not remove the consequences of your transgressions, He *will* remove His memory of them. If God has forgiven and forgotten, why not you? Because if you're holding on to a myriad of regrets about the past, you'll have no mind for the present, much less the future plans, God has for you. Not only that, but you may find yourself stuck or sick. Proverbs 28:13 (NLT) says, "People who conceal their sins will not prosper, but if they confess and turn from them, they will receive mercy."

Do you think your words of "forgive my trespasses as I forgive those who trespass against me" have fallen on deaf ears? Remember, God knows all your thoughts. He has heard your words and forgiven you "as far as the east is from the west" (Psalm 103:12 AMPC).

And so has Jesus. In fact, He died once and for all to save you from your sins! So turn away from your missteps and "turn to God so that your sins may be wiped out, that time after time your souls may know the refreshment that comes from the presence of God. Then he will send you Jesus" (Acts 3:19–20 PHILLIPS).

If you're having trouble getting there, have a talk with God about it—the God who says to you, "Come now, let's settle this. . . . Though your sins are like scarlet, I will make them as white as snow. Though they are red like crimson, I will make them as white as wool" (Isaiah 1:18 NLT).

After asking God's forgiveness—and *knowing* you've received it—forgive yourself. When you do, God not only will refresh and replenish you, wash you clean and get you back on your spiritual feet, but will strengthen you for the next task. Remember: "Anyone who belongs to Christ has become a new person. The old life is gone; a new life has begun!" (2 Corinthians 5:17 NLT). Grab that new life! Be well and move forward, in Jesus' name!

Lord Jesus, forgive my missteps. Forget what I've done in the past.
And help me to forgive myself so that You can begin a new thing
in me! Give me the confidence and courage I need to be
the new woman You created me to be! Amen!

Heart Treasure: In Jesus, I find self-forgiveness.

Finding Healing of Heart and Spirit

The Spirit of the Lord [is] upon Me, because He has anointed Me [the Anointed One, the Messiah] to preach the good news (the Gospel) to the poor; He has sent Me to announce release to the captives and recovery of sight to the blind, to send forth as delivered those who are oppressed [who are downtrodden, bruised, crushed, and broken down by calamity].

LUKE 4:18 AMPC

When you suffer a loss, you may find yourself dazed, walking around in a fog. Everything seems surreal. People ask you questions and you don't even hear their voices. You wonder, *How did this happen? What will I do now?*

The days pass and the fog lifts a bit, but not all the way. You begin to hear people's voices. Some try to console you by saying, "Time heals all wounds." And you don't know how to respond, so you just nod as if in agreement.

This state of shock you're in—whether it's from the death of a loved one, a foreclosed house, or the loss of a job you've had for years—does dissipate as the days go by. But time will not heal your wound. Only Jesus can do that.

When Jesus went to Nazareth where He grew up, He went to the synagogue, as He usually did on a Sabbath day. He stood up to read, and someone handed Him the book of Isaiah. He read the words of Isaiah 61:1–2, saying that the Spirit of the Lord was upon Him. That He was the Anointed One, the Messiah. That God had sent Him to preach the Good News to the poor, free the prisoners, give sight to the blind, and deliver those who were brokenhearted. That includes you.

So when you're in that fog of grief, when you can no longer hear people's voices, when their words bring you no comfort, go to the Lord, who will heal your broken heart and restore your crushed spirit (Psalm 34:18). Know that He is near, just a whisper away. He'll gather your tears (Psalm 56:8).

Your world may never be the same again, but you can count on God to never change. He will always be there. And someday you will smile again. Yes, it may take time, but God has all the time in the world to spend with you—just you. So cry on Jesus' shoulder. Let Him hold you close. Feel His heartbeat. Breathe in His peace and the warmth of His love.

Dear Lord Jesus, words escape me. I'm so filled with sorrow. But I know You're the One who heals me. You're the One who is always there, who will never leave me. So I come to You in this moment. Wrap Your love around me as I fall into Your arms. Amen.

Heart Treasure: In Jesus, I find healing of heart and spirit.

Finding the Fullness of Hope

I pray that God, the source of hope, will fill you completely with joy and peace because you trust in him. Then you will overflow with confident hope through the power of the Holy Spirit.

ROMANS 15:13 NLT

During times of hardship, we can find ourselves wondering why God has brought us such grief. We may even begin considering ourselves a victim of our circumstances. Soon a sense of hopelessness sets in. Wherever we go, we feel as if a dark cloud is hanging over us.

Naomi had this same woe-is-me mentality. She'd once lived in Bethlehem with her husband and two sons. When a famine came to their land, they moved to Moab where food was more plentiful. But then her husband died. Then her sons, who'd married Moabite women, also died.

When Naomi heard that the famine had ended in Bethlehem, she decided to return there, telling her two daughters-in-law to stay in Moab. When they tried to come with her, she said she was too old for a husband, and even if she did remarry and get pregnant, she said to them, "Would you wait for them to grow up and refuse to marry someone else? No, of course not, my daughters! Things are far more bitter for me than for you, because the LORD himself has raised his fist against me" (Ruth 1:13 NLT).

One daughter-in-law turned back, but the other, Ruth, was determined to go with Naomi. When they came into Bethlehem, the local women asked if Naomi was the woman they'd once known. She responded, "Call me not Naomi [pleasant]; call me Mara [bitter], for the Almighty has dealt very bitterly with me" (Ruth 1:20 AMPC). Then, "I went away full, but the LORD has brought me home empty. Why call me Naomi when the LORD has caused me to suffer and the Almighty has sent such tragedy upon me?" (Ruth 1:21 NLT).

Can you relate? Has your bitterness over life circumstances made you want to change your name from Once-Blessed to Woe-Is-Me? If so, you're missing what Naomi missed. The blessings you already have and the ones that lie ahead.

Naomi had Ruth, who would end up providing for her, marrying a rich man, and giving birth to a boy who would become, not just the grandfather of a king (David), but an ancestor of Jesus!

No matter what's happening in your life, don't bow to bitterness. Know that as a daughter of Father God, you are never a victim of your circumstances. He has a plan for your good! So hang on to the hope you have in Jesus. God will see you through!

Help me, Lord, to continually put my hope in You, no matter what my circumstances. For I know You will work out all things for my good. Thank You for the blessings I had yesterday, have today, and will have tomorrow.

Heart Treasure: In Jesus, I find the fullness of hope.

Finding a Favor-Filled Attitude

How exquisite your love, O God! How eager we are to run under
your wings, to eat our fill at the banquet you spread
as you fill our tankards with Eden spring water.
PSALM 36:7–8 MSG

How's your attitude? Defeatist or triumphant? Resigned or risen? When Naomi returned to Bethlehem with her daughter-in-law Ruth, they had nothing. Naomi even said she had left that land full and returned empty. But Ruth, who refused to leave Naomi's side in Moab (Ruth 1:16), had a different attitude. Because of her strong faith in God, her absolute trust that He'd take care of her, she was hopeful.

That's why, instead of allowing destitution to keep her down, she looked up. Her bright outlook, energy, determination, and assurance that all would be well, that God in His providence would provide, showed when she said to Naomi, "Let me go to the field and glean among the ears of grain after him in whose sight *I shall find favor*" (Ruth 2:2 ESV, emphasis added).

After Naomi granted Ruth permission to work in the fields, she immediately went out. And God showed His providence: "*And as it happened*, she found herself working in a field that belonged to Boaz" (Ruth 2:3 NLT, emphasis added). As it turned out, Boaz was the rich relation who would eventually marry Ruth and provide both her and Naomi with all they needed—and more!

Don't you love it when you step out, empty of all but energy, hopeful of God's providence, and things just start to "happen," to go in your favor?

Yet why was Boaz so kind to Ruth? Because he'd heard what she'd done. How she'd left her home and gods for the one true God and stuck to her mother-in-law's side. So he blessed her, saying, "The LORD repay you for what you have done, and a full reward be given you by the LORD, the God of Israel, under whose wings you have come to take refuge!"

(Ruth 2:12 ESV). After hearing these words from Boaz, Ruth said, "*I have found favor in your eyes*, my lord, for you have comforted me and spoken kindly to your servant" (Ruth 2:13 ESV, emphasis added).

When you trust in God's good providence, seek His refuge, deal kindly with others as Jesus has dealt with you, have a hopeful attitude, and use your energy to serve, putting your faith to work, you'll find favor in God's eyes as well as in the eyes of those around you.

Help me, Jesus, to gain that favor-filled attitude, to have a God-risen perspective, to use my energy to serve by putting my faith to work. As I seek refuge under Your wings and am kind to others, I know You'll help me find my way all my days. In Jesus' name I pray, amen.

Heart Treasure: In Jesus, I find a favor-filled attitude.

Finding Good Seeds to Sow

"Do to others whatever you would like them to do to you. This is the essence of all that is taught in the law and the prophets."
MATTHEW 7:12 NLT

*Y*ou're hurting. Someone said or did something that injured you. You feel like the innocent party in all of it. And maybe you are. But maybe you're not. Perhaps it's time to take stock, to consider what you may have been putting out there.

Jesus said we're to treat others the way we'd like to be treated. The apostle Paul took that idea even further in his letter to the Galatians, putting things in farmer's terms, words his readers would understand: "Do not be deceived: God is not mocked, for whatever one sows, that will he also reap. For the one who sows to his own flesh will from the flesh reap corruption, but the one who sows to the Spirit will from the Spirit reap eternal life" (Galatians 6:7–8 ESV).

So we reap what we sow. If we put out anger, chances are that's what we'll get back. Same with selfishness, hatred, envy, hard-heartedness, injustice, etc. You get the idea. So the question remains: What have you been sowing? Once you've reflected, let's consider what you should be putting out there, no matter who you're facing—friend, family, or foe.

For wisdom in dealing with others, we need to go to God in every situation. We need to ask Him what to say, how to respond so that we're sowing in the Spirit. For as James writes, "The wisdom from above is first of all pure. . .peace loving, gentle at all times, and willing to yield to others. . .full of mercy and the fruit of good deeds. . .shows no favoritism and is always sincere" (James 3:17 NLT). And what results will be reaped if we sow like this? "And those who are peacemakers will plant seeds of peace and reap a harvest of righteousness" (James 3:18 NLT).

Sounds like we'll need a lot of energy to sow all those good things in accordance with God's wisdom and in the Spirit. But with God's help, we will "not grow weary of doing good, for in due season we will reap, if we do not give up" (Galatians 6:9 ESV).

Like Jesus, we are to be good farmers so we can reap a good crop, a bounty of blessings for God, ourselves, and others. So plant those seeds of love and good deeds. When you do, you'll reap the benefits, in this life and the next.

Lord Jesus, sometimes I feel I may not be sowing as You would have me do. I let my non-spiritual side, circumstances, and button pushers get the best of me. Help me remember that I will reap what I sow. Help me plant love, forgiveness, peace, humility, gentleness, sincerity, and good deeds. In Your name, amen.

Heart Treasure: In Jesus, I find good seeds to sow.

Finding Supernatural Peace

"Sit back and relax, my dear daughter,
until we find out how things turn out."
RUTH 3:18 MSG

*W*aiting for exam results from a teacher or test results from a doctor's office can be torturous. Then there's that job interview. *Did they like me? Am I what they're looking for?* Perhaps you're waiting for another kind of answer. *Did I do well raising my kids? Have they turned out all right? . . . Did my boss like that report? . . . Will this new recipe be edible?*

In all these situations, you've taken certain actions. You've played your part. You've done all you can possibly do, to the best of your ability. And now you need to wait.

Naomi gives her daughter-in-law Ruth good advice. The young widow had put herself at Boaz's feet, under his protection. And he promised to marry her if her late husband's closer relative gave up his claim to her. So now all Ruth had to do was wait, "sit back and relax" until she saw how things panned out.

Waiting can be difficult. Even harder is doing it without worrying, without turning the situation over and over in your mind.

This is when your faith in Jesus can help you, when you benefit from falling back on your trust in God. This is when you remember the words of Romans 8:25 (AMPC): "If we hope for what is still unseen by us, we wait for it with patience and composure." And if you're not sure how to pray, offer your mumblings, sighs, moans to the Holy Spirit, who will help you out, bear up your prayers, and take them to God (Romans 8:26–27). This is when you remember that God will work out all things for your good (Romans 8:28). This is when you can get a new perspective on the situation by letting God know how grateful you are and leaving everything in His hands, regardless of the results: "Thank [God] in everything [no matter what the circumstances may be, be thankful and give thanks], for this is the will of God for you [who are] in Christ Jesus [the Revealer and Mediator of that will]" (1 Thessalonians 5:18 AMPC).

So, dear sister, about those answers, results, outcomes you're unsure of, the ones you're looking for, leave them in God's hands. Know He's working out the best solution for you and those around you. Then sit back and relax. All is well, and all will be well.

I'm not the most patient woman in the world, Lord Jesus. So I'm coming to You, bringing You all my worries and concerns, putting them at Your feet, knowing that whatever happens, the outcomes, the results, the scores are all in Your good hands. And so am I. And that's the best place to be. Thank You for being there, giving me rest and peace. Amen.

Heart Treasure: In Jesus, I find supernatural peace.

Finding the Strength to Stand Calm

But Moses told the people, "Don't be afraid. Just stand still and watch the LORD rescue you today. The Egyptians you see today will never be seen again. The LORD himself will fight for you. Just stay calm."
EXODUS 14:13–14 NLT

Some days you may be between a rock and a hard place, facing unbelievable odds or circumstances—within and without. You feel as if you're one of the Israelite women, standing with your kneading bowl bound up in your cloak on your shoulders. You're holding whatever food you can carry. Your children are clinging to your cloak. Your husband is standing with the flocks or clutching the bag of silver and gold jewelry and clothes handed over by the Egyptians you left behind.

You're standing at the shore of the Red Sea. Suddenly, over the roar of the waters, you hear the thunderous hooves of horses and wheels of chariots. It's Pharaoh coming with over six hundred chariots to bring you back from your brief respite from slavery. There is nowhere to go.

And then you hear your godly leader, Moses, a type of Christ. He tells you not to panic. To just stand still and watch what God does. You'll never see this enemy again. God is going to fight this battle for *you*. So just. . .stay. . .calm.

The same words come ringing through for God's people in 2 Chronicles 20:15 (NLT): "This is what the LORD says: Do not be afraid! Don't be discouraged by this mighty army, for the battle is not yours, but God's."

It all sounds good. Stuff you can really sink your teeth—not to mention your heart and mind—into. But how do you get from chaotic emotions to calm ones? You turn to the wisdom of Ephesians 6:10–11 (MSG): "God is strong, and he wants you strong. So take everything the Master has set out for you, well-made weapons of the best materials. And put them to use so you will be able to stand up to everything the Devil throws your way."

So you dress up in the weapons God has provided, including but not limited to the breastplate of righteousness, the belt of truth, the shoes of peace, the shield of faith, the sword of the Spirit, which is the Word of God (Ephesians 6:14–17).

When you do, the fear fades, the peace resounds, the faith builds, the Word protects, and the truth prevails, enabling you to stand, be calm, be still, and watch God work.

Jesus, help me look to You in the midst of whatever battles I'm facing, within and without. I know that in You and with God's armor, I can stand. And praise. Thank You for these truths and the strength and protection You and Your Word provide. In Your name I pray, amen.

Heart Treasure: In Jesus, I find the strength to stand calm.

Finding the Solid Rock

"If. . .a helpless man. . .was healed. . .it was done in the name of Jesus Christ of Nazareth! . . . It is by his power that this man at our side stands in your presence perfectly well. He is the 'stone which was rejected by you builders, which has become the chief cornerstone.' "
ACTS 4:9–11 PHILLIPS

What-ifs can drive a woman crazy. *What if I don't have the strength for this day? What if I make the wrong decision? What if Fate has other plans for me? What if this person isn't telling me the truth? What if my plans don't work out?*

If you attempt to base your life on earthly what-if thoughts, your foundation is going to be shaky. God would like you to exchange your earthly what-ifs for thoughts with a more spiritual slant.

Consider how your feelings change when you do a heavenly reframe. *What if you count on the fact that God will give you the strength you need for this day? What if you believe that God will help you make the right decision? What if you realize you're not at the mercy of Fate but are being led by God in a definite way? What if you lean on the fact that God can read people's hearts and minds and will lead you to the truth of all matters? What if you trust that God has plans for you and nothing can stand in their way?*

God wants you to know that although He's the architect of your life, you're the builder. And He wants you to have your foundation on Jesus Christ. He wants you to embrace Jesus, to make Him your chief cornerstone. God wants you and your life rooted in Christ, grounded in Him (Colossians 2:7; Ephesians 3:17).

God knows exactly what you need—and exactly when you need it. He's moving things and people in and out of your way. He's planning a specific future, has a specific purpose for you. But your life with Him will not be solid until you replace those weakening earthly what-ifs with definite spiritual affirmations of God's power and strength for living.

Each time an earthly what-if comes into your mind, capture it in Christ's power and replace it with an affirmation of God's power working within you through Jesus and the Holy Spirit. By doing so, you'll have a Rock-solid foundation on which to build your life.

Lord Jesus, I want You to be the foundation of my life. Help me weed out those weakening what-if stones and replace them with You, my solid Rock. Remind me that with Father God as my architect, I'm constructing a forever building in His kingdom. Amen.

Heart Treasure: In Jesus, I find the solid Rock of my life.

Finding God's Spirit and Christ Within

I pray that from his glorious, unlimited resources he will empower you
with inner strength through his Spirit. Then Christ will make his
home in your hearts as you trust in him. Your roots will
grow down into God's love and keep you strong.
EPHESIANS 3:16–17 NLT

No matter how weak you may feel in physical strength, you have another strength you can pull from within. No matter how ill-prepared or lacking you may feel, you have access to amazing resources, ones unlimited and eternal, through God, His Spirit, and Jesus Christ!

God has all the resources you could ever want to help you live your life for Him, to do good, to help others, to overcome whatever troubles appear, to eliminate whatever obstacles stand in your way—no matter how large, ominous, and looming they look to your earthly eyes. God will empower you with strength from within. Through His Spirit residing in your inner woman, "Himself indwelling your innermost being and personality" (Ephesians 3:16 AMPC), you can overcome anything that stands in the way of God's plans for your life!

And the more you trust Jesus to see you through, the more you count on Him paving that pathway to God, the more you realize how much of your strength and power and love is really His, the more Christ will grow in your heart. But it takes faith, a firm belief that He's there: "May Christ *through your faith* [actually] dwell (settle down, abide, make His permanent home) in your hearts!" (Ephesians 3:17 AMPC, emphasis added).

Through your faith and trust that Christ dwells within your heart, you build a fortress that will always be there for you to deliver you in times of intense distress. Psalm 9:9 (ESV) tells you that "the LORD is a stronghold for the oppressed, a stronghold in times of trouble." Christ is that stronghold!

Live your life with that knowledge. Lean into the strength of God's Spirit ensconced in your inner woman. Meditate on the truth that the Son of God who healed diseases, stilled the waves, stopped the storm, and so much more has settled Himself down in your heart. Recognize the ways in which the Spirit and Christ are there for you. Become more and more aware of not only their presence and power within you but how they're working things out in your life.

Then you'll be rooted in all the love that secures and empowers your walk with God.

Oh, thank You so much, God, for planting Your Spirit in my inner woman and Christ within my heart, giving me all the strength and power I need. Jesus is my stronghold, the One I rely on in times of trouble, leading me to the love that secures my walk and life. Amen.

Heart Treasure: In Jesus, I find God's Spirit and Christ within me.

Finding Your Way Back to Father God

*"And while he was still a long way off, his father saw him coming.
Filled with love and compassion, he ran to his son,
embraced him, and kissed him."*

LUKE 15:20 NLT

It can become exhausting trying to live in our own power, to adhere to our own wisdom. At times we may breathe out a quick prayer, a "Help me, Jesus," but then we go back to working in what little human strength we have left. Or we read a quick devotion before beginning our day, but its meaning is soon lost in the busyness of our schedules. When will we come to our senses and truly live in Father God?

In Luke 15:11–32, the younger of two sons asks for what he'd inherit upon his father's demise, is given it, then goes out and spends it. He's soon destitute, eating pig slop. Then "he finally [comes] to his senses" (Luke 15:17 NLT) and returns to his father. While he's still a far way off, his expectantly waiting dad sees him coming. Brimming over with love and compassion, the father runs to his son, hugging and kissing him. Before the son even gets out everything he wants to tell his dad, his father tells the servants, "Bring the finest robe in the house and put it on him. Get a ring for his finger and sandals for his feet" (Luke 15:22 NLT). Then he orders a feast to be prepared to celebrate the son's return.

God is waiting expectantly, full of love and compassion, for you to return. He sees you trying to live your life with those things He's already blessed you with. Yet you're doing so at a distance from Him. And you're discovering a hunger that cannot be satisfied by the things of this world.

Return to Father God with all your heart and attention. Jesus has paved the way for you to have an amazing relationship with Him. God wants to feed you with His wisdom, clothe you with His grace, shod you with His strength, and engage you once again as His daughter.

Come to your senses. Ask Father God what He wants to tell you. Read the Bible until its words feed your soul. Then write those words down. Meditate on them and turn them into a prayer. Carry them in your spirit throughout the day. And soon you will find yourself once again enveloped in Father God's love and compassion.

Lord Jesus, I've strayed from Father God's Word and wisdom. I've been trying to live this life in my own strength. And I am hungry for real food. Come with me now as I enter God's Word. Help me to feel His love and compassion and to fall into His open arms as I begin my journey back to Him. In Your name I pray, amen.

Heart Treasure: In Jesus, I find my way back to Father God.

Finding Amazing Hope

When everything was hopeless, Abraham believed anyway,
deciding to live not on the basis of what he saw he
couldn't do but on what God said he would do.
ROMANS 4:18 MSG

hank God for His Word because it contains amazing stories of hope. Abraham is a great example of one who didn't ever give up on God or His promises. He knew that God could create something out of nothing. And he dared to believe in God's promise—"to trust God to do what only God could do. . .with a word make something out of nothing" (Romans 4:17 MSG)—to make him a father of many.

God's promise to Abraham must have seemed like an impossibility! For both Abraham and his wife Sarah were very old, well beyond childbearing years. But God made what seemed impossible—an elderly couple having a son—possible.

Romans 4:20–21 (AMPC) goes on to say: "No unbelief or distrust made him waver (doubtingly question) concerning the promise of God, but he grew strong and was empowered by faith as he gave praise and glory to God, fully satisfied and assured that God was able and mighty to keep His word and to do what He had promised."

Do you see that? Even in the midst of what seemed like a hopeless scenario, Abraham never wavered in his trust in the promise God had made. But he grew stronger and more empowered by his faith! And he did so by giving praise and glory to God—before he received the promise! He could do that because he was fully convinced God would come through—as promised!

How's your faith in the midst of hopelessness? How convinced are you that God will come through on His promises?

When Solomon built the temple for God, he built two pillars. He named the south pillar Jachin, which means "He establishes," and the north pillar Boaz, which means "in Him is strength" (see 2 Chronicles 3:17). Know that God can create something out of nothing and that in Him is all the strength you need.

Abraham's faith in God's promises made him right with God. And we too can be right "when we embrace and believe the One who brought Jesus to life when the conditions were equally hopeless" (Romans 4:24 MSG). God gives you promises and hope. Believe that He can make something out of nothing and that in Him is your strength.

I believe in You, Jesus. And in God's promises. I believe He can make something out of nothing with just a look, a word, a breath. I praise God, giving Him glory and honor for what He is going to do in my life. And as I wait, my faith grows ever stronger! Amen!

Heart Treasure: In Jesus, I find amazing hope.

Finding Calmness in Waiting

"Staying with it—that's what God requires.
Stay with it to the end. You won't be sorry, and you'll be saved."
MATTHEW 24:13 MSG

In this world of instant gratification, you may find it hard to wait. Impatience, frustration, and anxiety can set in when you arrive at the doctor's office ten minutes before your appointment and find the waiting room full of people. . .waiting. The same emotions can flood in when you're waiting for a response to an email or phone call to a prospective employer, home buyer, or money lender. Perhaps you're overwhelmed with worry when waiting for a loved one to get home from the office or school on a snowy day.

It may even be that emotions set off by your impatience have put you off prayer. You've been asking God for something for hours, days, weeks, months, maybe even years. And no response, no answer yet. But Jesus wants you to stick with those prayers—and with God. When you do, you won't be sorry.

Perhaps the reason you haven't had an answer is that you aren't praying in God's will. It could be that God has already responded but you don't yet see the results because He's lining things up for you. It may be that you haven't really asked Him for what you truly want or haven't been asking right (James 4:2–3). Perhaps God wants to work within you. He wants to build up your character, your trust in Him. He wants your heart, mind, body, soul, and spirit to be ready for His answer. It may even be that you've already received an answer but aren't accepting it.

So what do you do in the meantime? Keep praying. Keep going until you and God narrow things down and discover what you should truly be praying for. And keep hoping. Expect that God will answer. It may not be the answer you want to hear, but you will get an answer.

After Jesus was resurrected by the power of the God of impossibilities,

He was sharing a meal with His followers. "He commanded them not to leave Jerusalem but to wait for what the Father had promised" (Acts 1:4 AMPC). And what did they do in the meantime? They "devoted themselves steadfastly to prayer, [waiting together] with the women" (Acts 1:14 AMPC).

So keep waiting. Keep calm in your faith, trusting God will deliver as promised. And keep praying expectantly. God *will* answer.

Jesus, help me grow in this period of waiting. Show me how to pray for God's way. Build up my patience, my hope, my expectancy. I'm leaning on You, knowing You and the Spirit will work in me to give me the right words, the ones that will carry to God's ears. In Your name I pray, amen.

Heart Treasure: In Jesus, I find calmness in waiting.

Finding Words of Pure Gold

*Post this at all the intersections, dear friends: Lead with your ears,
follow up with your tongue, and let anger straggle along in the
rear. God's righteousness doesn't grow from human anger.*
JAMES 1:19–20 MSG

You've done it again. You've said something you shouldn't have. The words were out of your mouth before you had a chance to stop them. And now you're feeling bad. You realize you hurt not only someone else but yourself and Jesus in the process! For He talked of loving others and doing good, and you've done the opposite.

How does this happen? How do these words just spill out? And what do those words, ones that tear down instead of building up, tell others about your walk with Jesus?

Well, what's been going *into* you is just what's coming *out*. As Jesus said, "Listen, and take this to heart. It's not what you swallow that pollutes your life, but what you vomit up" (Matthew 15:11 MSG).

Hmm. Perhaps you've had too much of the pollution of the world coming into your life and not enough of the Word. You're at the point where you can't even hear or recognize God's voice! It's time to listen up.

American lay minister S. D. Gordon has some good advice in this regard. He writes, "God speaks in His Word. The most we know of God comes to us here. This Book is God in print. God Himself speaks in this Book. Studying it keenly, intelligently, reverently will reveal God's great will. What He says will utterly change what you say."

God's Word will "utterly change what you say." Those are some words that need to sink in deep—along with God's Word, of course. But don't stop there. "*Act* on what you hear!" (James 1:22 MSG, emphasis added).

When you embed yourself in God's Word, when you actually do what it says—loving others as you love yourself, building them up, encouraging them—you'll more likely find yourself holding your tongue in check or saying exactly what God wants you to say in each situation. For God will either give you the power to remain silent or create for your tongue words that are beautiful, wise, and life affirming. And God will utterly change not just what you say to others but what you say to yourself as well. He'll change up the monologue of your inner critic or silence her altogether.

So go to God's Word. Study it. Memorize it. Make it part of the fabric of your very being. Let God's words utterly change your own.

Help me be humble enough to apologize to those I have spoken to in anger, Jesus. And walk with me as I become not just a reader of God's Word but a doer. Help me walk as You walked, speak as You spoke, love as You loved, in word and deed. Amen.

Heart Treasure: In Jesus, I find words of pure gold.

Finding Freedom from Doubt and Despair

"You will have complete and free access to God's kingdom,
keys to open any and every door: no more barriers
between heaven and earth, earth and heaven."
MATTHEW 16:19 MSG

loved one is ill. A child lost. A teenager walking down a dark path. A parent dying. A friend divorcing. A house flooding.

All these happenings can leave you reeling. In the beginning you think you'll have the strength to navigate your way through or to help those who right now can't seem to help themselves. But then one day you find yourself going down, beginning to have doubts, which lead to despair.

These words, *doubt* and *despair*, have interesting etymologies. The Online Etymology Dictionary says the verb *doubt* in the early thirteenth century meant "to dread, fear." It derives from the Latin word *dubitare*, "to question, hesitate, waver in opinion." It's about being torn between two things. Sounds torturous, doesn't it? *Despair*, according to the Online Etymology Dictionary, derives from the Latin word *desperare*, "to lose all hope."

In John Bunyan's Christian allegory *The Pilgrim's Progress*, the character Christian has been beaten, tortured, and imprisoned by the Giant Despair in Doubting Castle. In the dark dungeon, bemoaning his situation, Christian has an epiphany. He remembers a key he has. Its name? Promise! That key of promise ends up opening every lock in the doors of Doubting Castle, freeing our hero! As he ran, not even the Giant Despair could chase him down because the giant found his limbs unable to move, enabling Christian to find his way back to the King's highway and then to safety!

You too have such a key! You too can be such a hero! You have loads of promises in God's Word that can free you from the chains, the imprisonment, the weight of doubt and despair! Try these keys and see if they fit in the lock:

- "If you remain in me and my words remain in you, you may ask for anything you want, and it will be granted!" (John 15:7 NLT).
- "God will make this happen, for he who calls you is faithful" (1 Thessalonians 5:24 NLT).
- "God's way is perfect. All the Lord's promises prove true. He is a shield for all who look to him for protection" (Psalm 18:30 NLT).

If these promises don't open the door to your castle of doubt and free you from the giant of despair, start searching the Bible for ones that will fit the lock. When you do, you'll find your freedom.

I'm longing for my freedom, Jesus. I'm grasping for, then holding on to, the key of Your promises to me. I'm going to use them to unlock the doors that have me imprisoned by doubt and despair. And as I go through those doors, I'm running for Your highway, Your path to faith and joy! In Jesus' name I pray, amen!

Heart Treasure: In Jesus, I find freedom from doubt and despair.

Finding God's Choice

*By faith, Noah built a ship in the middle of dry land. He was warned about
something he couldn't see, and acted on what he was told. The result?
His family was saved. His act of faith drew a sharp line between the
evil of the unbelieving world and the rightness of the believing
world. As a result, Noah became intimate with God.*

HEBREWS 11:7 MSG

Each moment of every day you find yourself having to make a choice.
Do you turn right or left out of the driveway? Wear a coat or not?
Buy a new purse or save the money? Peruse the morning paper or God's
Word? Watch reality TV or read a story to the kids? And each decision
you make may bring you closer to or remove you further from God and
His plan for you.

Remember Noah? He had a choice. He could either believe that God
was going to flood the earth or not. If he believed, he'd have to build that
enormous ark, load his family and creatures inside, then wait for rain. If
he didn't believe, he wouldn't be mocked by his neighbors, but he, his
family, and God's land creatures would die in the massive flood. Noah
chose to believe God. And because of that, he was led into an intimate
relationship with Him.

Where have your choices been leading you?

Jesus asks you to walk with Him. To come away with Him and find
ease, comfort, and joy for your life. He asks you to plead with your Father
God as He did, saying, "Lord, not my will but Yours be done." And then
head down that path with Him, closer and closer to the One who has your
best interests—and the world's best interests—in His heart and mind.

By faith, choose God's will for your life. Decide this day whom you
will serve (Joshua 24:15–16).

God says, "Now listen! Today I am giving you a choice between life
and death, between prosperity and disaster" (Deuteronomy 30:15 NLT).

If you choose to love Jesus and keep His commands, walking the way He walked, "you will live and multiply, and the LORD your God will bless you and the land you are about to enter and occupy" (Deuteronomy 30:16 NLT). That means He'll bless every step you take, each place you walk. And you'll become more and more like the Son of Man He sent to help you find your way.

What will you choose today?

Lord Jesus, help me stop at each intersection of my life and choose the path God would have me take. When I do, whether that road be hard or easy, I know I'll be on the right path and heading ever closer to You and the rich life You offer. Amen.

Heart Treasure: In Jesus, I find God's choice.

Encouraging and Practical Journals for Your Quiet Time

My Bible Study Journal: Peace for My Anxious Heart
This great journal features Bible reading plans that will encourage you to experience more fully the peace of Jesus, as you learn to trust Him more fully. It's perfect for your own personal quiet time or small group study!

Spiral Bound / 978-1-64352-862-5 / $9.99

Discovering God in Everyday Moments Devotional Journal
Here is a delightful devotional journal that celebrates the presence of the heavenly Father in life's everyday moments. 180 thought-provoking readings will speak to your heart, sharing spiritual truths from God's Word.

Spiral Bound / 978-1-64352-729-1 / $9.99